Reaching For Reality

Reaching For Reality

Reaching For Reality

Seven Incredible True Stories
of Alien Abduction

Constance Clear, M.A., M.S.W.

Consciousness Now, Inc.
San Antonio, TX

Reaching For Reality

Seven Incredible True Stories of Alien Abduction

By Constance Clear, M.A., M.S.W.

Published by:
Consciousness Now, Inc.
P.O. Box 15994
San Antonio, TX 78212
Printed in the United States of America

Publisher's Cataloging In Publication
(Provided by Quality Books, Inc.)

Clear, Constance.
    Reaching for reality : seven incredible true
stories of alien abduction / Constance Clear. -- 1st
ed.
        p. cm.
        Includes index.
        LCCN: 98-92297
        ISBN: 0-9667053-1-9

    1. Unidentified flying objects--Sightings and
encounters. 2. Abduction. I. Title.

TL789.3.C54 1999   001.9′42
                                    QBI98-1696

*Seven survivors of alien
abduction share their first-hand
accounts so others will know...*

You are not alone.

Author's Note:

Confidentiality between therapist and client is a time-honored principle of social work ethics. The clients who wrote the following stories have authorized me to publish their writings and to share my professional observations regarding my work with them. Only their names and some identifying details have been altered to protect their privacy.

A portion of the sale proceeds of this book will be donated to further research and awareness regarding alien abduction.

Acknowledgments

This project has unfolded as though it were being orchestrated by some invisible force. I feel honored to have witnessed and compiled these amazing stories for you, the reader.

To Kay, Lydia, Daniel, Theresa, Andrew, Maggie, and Sara, who share their innermost selves in these pages, no words can adequately convey the immense gratitude and respect I feel for each of you. I also want to recognize your loved ones for their input, and emotional support.

A special word of gratitude is conveyed to John Mack, M.D., David Jacobs, Ph.D., John Lerma, M.D., and Whitley and Anne Strieber for the parts each of you played in this unfolding drama and for the help each of you have given me.

This book could not have been brought into being without the skillful help of Walt and Marcy Bashore, Phil Pennington of Image Networks. I am also grateful to Joy Bunch, Jennifer Martin, Geri Gregory, Dave Stamper, Lucinda and David Frost, Stacy Pennington, and Lynda Stannard for their assistance with the manuscript. For the cover design, I would like to thank Lydia who drew the hands, and Trustin Clear and John Potts for the design. Lastly, I want to thank my husband, Brent Fisher, for his encouragement to move forward with this project.

Contents

Reaching For Reality

Introduction

The Reluctant Co-Therapist

Have you ever looked up into a night sky full of stars and had a feeling of homesickness sweep over you? Deep in your soul do you want to believe we're not alone, or are you one of those people who dread going to bed at night because you *know* we're not alone?

This book was not compiled to convince you that alien abduction exists, but rather to give voice to those forced to live with such realities. The following stories are the first-hand accounts of seven survivors of alien abduction. What are the odds that these seven people, each living within two hundred miles of San Antonio, Texas and each having maintained silence regarding his or her suspected lifelong involvement with alien abduction, would decide to seek professional help and would end up in my office within fourteen months of each other?

Working with these courageous men and women has been the most challenging, disturbing, and transforming experience of my twenty-nine year career as a psychotherapist. Not only have I had to endure the shock of having my world view radically altered, but I've had to contend with the fear that doing this work would increase my chances of having an alien encounter. I certainly understand why so few mental health professionals have become involved in this area of study.

Soon after beginning my work with these clients, I realized that though they were deriving benefit from their individual sessions with me, what they needed most was to be able to interact with each other. I started a support group for them which later became known as the Friday Night Group. Upon meeting such credible peers, each of the group members felt validated. Through the lively and compassionate group interaction they found the inner strength to face their ongoing experiences more consciously and their fears began to diminish.

1

I asked my clients to write about their experiences, in hopes that it would help them work through their feelings. Though they found it difficult to reveal things they had learned to keep secret, each of them reported a sense of relief in doing so. The idea that their stories might help others gave meaning to their harrowing experiences. I am grateful to each of the contributors for their willingness to make their stories public, thus allowing me to speak out on their behalf. I have presented their stories in the order that the individuals found their way to me. It should be noted that the contributors did not read each other's stories until the book was finished.

These are the stories of ordinary people. Though two of them are married to each other, the rest met for the first time through me. Their ages range from the twenties to the sixties, and their politics range from liberal democrats to conservative republicans. Six of the seven are married, four have children, and one has grandchildren. Their educational backgrounds include education, computer programming, drafting, mathematics, linguistics, and counseling. Four of them are public school teachers, one works in the aircraft industry and two are currently staying home raising young children.

For personal and/or professional reasons, the contributors to this book have chosen to remain anonymous. Although their names have been changed, their stories have not been altered. It is of particular interest to me to observe how differently each of these individuals has reacted to his or her circumstances. While the women have become more or less reconciled to the periodic intrusions into their lives, the men continue to express their resolve to kill their captors if given the chance.

Five of my seven clients requested hypnosis to aid in recovery of repressed memories. Four of them achieved excellent results but one was unable to stay in trance long enough to derive benefit. Though all of them reported some symptoms of anxiety, depression, or post-traumatic stress, none displayed psychotic features, fit the criteria for a personality disorder, or had a history of childhood abuse.

As for me, I feel as though I've become a co-therapist to an alien intelligence that doesn't care that I object to their treatment plan. Perhaps it's easier for the aliens to keep their subjects amnesiac regarding their visits, but it certainly is not in the best interest of the humans involved. Keeping traumatic experiences out of conscious awareness is like holding a basketball under water. It takes a lot of effort, and if you let go, you're in trouble. Imagine what it would be like to live with periods of missing time, to wake up with unexplained marks on your body, and to experience flashbacks so bizarre that you don't mention them to anyone.

If you are having similar experiences, I hope that reading this book will bring you validation. If nothing like this has ever happened to you, you have the luxury of dismissing the subject, but please don't. You never know when a friend, or family member might lean over and say, "I've never told anyone this before, but..."

Chapter One

Driven to the Edge

Prologue to Kay's Story

This book would not exist were it not for Kay. During her first session she looked at me and said, "Someone needs to write a self-help book for people like me." I heard myself offering to help. A year and a half later my mother died and I inherited the task of having her book, *Not My Will*, published in the Philippines. The prospect of publishing a book no longer seemed frightening and by then, I had seven clients with incredible stories to tell.

From the beginning, this book has had a life of its own. I am especially grateful to Kay for initiating the idea. It seems only fitting that our story should begin with her. Kay is an intelligent, happily married woman in her late thirties who is unable to have children. When I first met her she was considering adopting a child, but as she realized the extent of her involvement with her night visitors she decided it would not be right to bring a child into her world. This was a painful decision for Kay and her husband, Rafael, to make.

Kay first came to see me in February of 1995. Over the next three and a half years, I saw her 25 times, with most of the sessions lasting two hours. During some sessions, hypnosis was utilized to explore conscious memory fragments or material that, at first, appeared to be a dream. It has been my practice to allow my clients to select whether and when to use hypnosis.

During our early hypnotic regressions, Kay periodically experienced a severe burning sensation in her elbows, which seemed to function as an impediment to remembering. After a few sessions, Kay suddenly announced that she had lost all interest in UFOs, and although she saw me for a couple of subsequent sessions, she focused her attention on other matters. Weeks later, Kay had another

5

encounter, and she returned, motivated to resume our uncovering work. From that point on, her response to hypnosis deepened. Once in trance, it was as though she reentered a familiar world, and she verbalized less and less of what she recalled.

At some point, she realized that the same being had been working with her throughout her life. The love she felt for this being seemed to diminish the fear associated with her abductions, and she began to express an intense longing to return to her home in the stars. The anguish she felt living between her two worlds intensified and Rafael, who occasionally joined us for a session, lived with the gnawing fear that his wife would be taken and not returned.

For a time, Kay was forced to quit working, as she would awaken exhausted several mornings in a row. It was interesting to note that her two cats, who normally slept with her, would not come into her bedroom on the nights she was visited. Finally, one day on her way home from an appointment with me, she was so distraught that she tried to throw herself from the car, traveling 70 miles per hour. Luckily, Rafael was able to grab her in time. Two nights later, Kay was to have an experience that would bring her peace. It was as though the aliens knew she was at the end of her tolerance, and they intervened.

Kay's Account: Written December 1996

To start my story, I would like to talk about why I've decided to write this. In the summer of 1994, the activity from the aliens started up again. It had been quite a few years since I'd heard from them, about 16 or 17 years since my last memory of them. My first thought was "Here we go again, they're back". Accepting them into my life was the last thing I wanted to do. While the childhood years were fun, my teenage years were frightening, to say the least, and I did not want a repeat of those years. As the weeks went by, and the visits became more frequent, I knew this was something that could not be ignored. My job and my sanity were in jeopardy. Something had to be done, and soon.

The town I live in is small, and there was no one I could turn to for help without being thought of as mentally ill. Telling my husband or any family members was out of the question. After a disturbing experience one night, I went to the book store to try and find something to help explain what was happening to me. I ended up with a book that told the stories of several people who were having experiences like mine. In the back of the book, was the author's address. I wrote to the author, pleading for help. He sent me a list of therapists in the area. I made an appointment with the one closest to me, and started seeing her.

After over a year of therapy, I've learned how to integrate these experiences back into my life in a positive way. That feeling of despair of not having anyone to talk to was something that will always be remembered. If I had not found that book to read, there is no telling what might have happened to me. If what I write here helps just one person, then it will have been worth my while to have written it.

There are a few things I would like to touch on before describing my experiences:

Physical symptoms and unusual medical history:

At the age of 15, I discovered a scar above my navel. The scar is about 1 inch long and slanted sideways. It was near dinner time and my mother was cooking supper. I walked into the kitchen and asked my mother if I had surgery when I was little. She said no without turning around from what she was doing. I said, "But what about this scar on my stomach?" She turned around with a panicked look on her face and said, "There is no scar. It's just your imagination." From her reaction, I decided it was best not to ask any more questions.

I am unable to have children because of so much scar tissue in my reproductive area.

Psychological symptoms:

When I was a little girl, I had trouble concentrating, and was very shy and withdrawn. I always wanted to just blend in with everyone. I didn't want to stand out. It was very important to me to be normal even though I knew I wasn't like other people.

Many times, I would dream of having ghosts in my room at night, or spacemen, as I would call them. When I tried to tell my mother, she would tell me it was my imagination, or to just pray about it and they would go away. Well, they never went away.

As a teenager, when I came into my reproductive years, the dreams of ghosts/aliens turned into nightmares. I hated all of them during those years. I drank a lot to try to forget. One night I was with a group of friends. We were just a group of girls getting together to have a few drinks, and do some male bashing. As usual, I drank too much. I was sitting in a room alone, trying to go to sleep, when a friend of mine came into the room, and turned on the light. She said I was hysterical, and screaming about the lights. I remember the panic of seeing the bright light overhead. Friends of mine always thought it was strange how sensitive I was to bright lights. They always sent me into a panic.

My first encounter memory is of when I was 6 months old. I am now 38 years old, and two years ago was the first time I was able to talk about my memories to anyone. First to my husband, and then a therapist. The therapist I see is open-minded, and wonderful to work with. With the help of my loving husband, and my therapist, I was able to save my sanity. I felt like I was going to break down at any minute or commit suicide. They have helped me learn how to live with this, and with who I am. Just recently, I summoned up the nerve to talk to my older brother, and his wife about it, and found out he has also had alien experiences. He has a scoop mark in the front of his leg, just like the ones described by countless other experiencers. I plan to talk more about abductions, the next time we see each other. Right now, I am trying to find a way to tell the rest of the family about my experiences. The support group I belong to is nice. There a person can talk, and no one will judge you. My husband doesn't feel comfortable in the group. He isn't ready to talk about this in front of people. That's OK with me. I would never push him into a situation which made him feel uncomfortable.

I'd like to tell about my experiences as I remember them, starting with the first one I can remember.

6 Months: When I opened my eyes, I could see my baby crib. It was square shaped, and made of a light colored wood. I looked to my right, and there he was, one of the aliens. He wasn't very tall. The railing of the bed reached him below the neck. He didn't have a hard time looking in. His hands were on the railing as he looked in. His fingers were long and thin. He stayed there awhile just checking on how I was coming along.

6-8 Years-old: When I awoke, there was someone beside my bed. It was one of them again. He said to come with him because he was going to take me to play on the ship. My first thought was that it would be fun to go. As I stepped beside him, he put his right arm around me and we floated off the floor. We were headed toward the window of the next room when my parents came out of their bedroom. My mother was screaming at my father not to let him take me. I looked back over my shoulder as he did something that froze my parents. They were like statues. He told me they would be fine, and not to worry about them.

After leaving the house, I looked down and could see the tops of the trees in our yard. We went up through the bottom of the ship. The bottom of the ship was so black. The blackest black color I've ever seen. After we were in, he sat me down at something that is similar to the computers we have today. He said it was just an aptitude test and to just think of it as a game. After doing that for awhile, we went for a walk. He took my left hand, and we started walking down a corridor. As we walked along. he told me they had to wait awhile to come for me, because they wanted me to be able to understand what they had to say, and they would not have to watch me as closely as they would a smaller child. We stopped and looked at something. When I looked to my right, I could see a round railing. In the middle was light going up and down. There are no walls. In the middle of the light was an object floating on its own power. It looked like two prisms in the shape of pyramids and the two prisms were put together at the base. The object was spinning around and giving off different colors as it spun around. It was very pretty. He didn't tell me what it was. He continued talking, saying that he wanted me to know where I came from. He said the line of people I come from are engineers and that they are a royal line, so that would make me a little princess. He told me some other things, but I don't remember everything he said. He felt so familiar to me. Like I had always known him. There isn't much more of that experience that I remember.

There is something that did happen about two years ago that I believe was connected to this incident. My father was talking with a friend of his about guns. A family friend had just purchased her first hunting gun. My father was telling his friend about how he used to sleep with a gun when he and my mom were first married. I was five when they married. He said that one night, he woke up standing in the living room, with his gun in his hand, not remembering how he got there. My mom was with him, saying she had heard something, and she made him get out of bed to check it out. My mom said she just remembers hearing something in the living room. As he was telling his story, I had flashes of what happened that night, and all of the incidents came flooding back. I plan to talk to my parents about this one day. Getting up the nerve is another thing. It may be quite soon, though, because my father suffers from panic attacks, and they may be related in some way to that incident.

8-14 Years-old: In those years, there were other abductions, but I have little memory of them, just bits and pieces of times I know were abductions. One night, I saw tiny white tornadoes in my grandmother's front yard. I have always associated that with the abductions. In July of 1996, I talked about this for the first time with my older brother. Before I could mention the white tornadoes, he asked me if I remembered the white tornadoes in our grandmother's front yard. I was stunned. He had confirmed what I had seen. I was too shocked to say anything more or ask questions. I talked about the therapy I was going through, and how it has helped me. I have yet to call him to talk some more about our childhood experiences. He seems reluctant to say anything. I'll give him a while longer and see if he comes around. We live 600 miles apart, and we won't be seeing each other for about a year. I guess I'll have to shop around for a good long distance company when we do start talking about this.

On another night, I was riding in the passenger seat of my mother's car. My mother was driving. As we drove along the dark road, I was looking out the window at the night sky. It was a clear night, and it seemed like I could see all the stars in the universe. A feeling of homesickness came over me. This feeling is something I can still remember and feel. I remember thinking that if I didn't go home soon my heart was going to break. The home I wanted to go to was up there somewhere among the stars. For a moment I was confused, not knowing why I was here and for what purpose. I silently cried, not letting my mother see. There was no way I could explain how I was feeling. Besides, she always told me that the things I saw at night were just my imagination or a dream.

15-19 Years-old: During these years, there was a lot of activity. I was continually questioning my existence. Why was I here and where did I come from? I knew that I was part of the aliens. A part of me wanted to know everything and another part of me wanted nothing to do with them. Sometimes, I felt like a game piece on a chess board, and the players lived somewhere away from Earth.

One night, my brother and I, and two of our friends, were driving in the family car. We were taking one of our friends home. She lived on a farm about 5 miles outside of town. About a mile from her house, my brother stopped the car and said, "Look out the window, there is something in the sky." We looked to our right, and saw a huge round ship rise up above the tree tops. The other girl and I started screaming. The two boys in the car said they wanted to go back to town to get the police. The friend we were taking home wanted to go to her house. She was afraid "they" had done something to her family. The next thing I knew, the car was quiet, and the other three people in the car were not moving. When I looked out of the window, there were four aliens. They opened the door, and told me to come along with them. I started screaming as I was getting out of the car. I felt like I was being forced out mentally. One of them turned around, and told me to stop screaming. He was irritated with me, and said for me to stop causing so much trouble, as it would only delay the procedures. They were on a tight schedule, and didn't have time to spend with a screaming person, who knew what was going on, and why it was happening. When he said that, I calmed down and stopped screaming, but I did pout until they brought me back. That was the only time in my thirty-nine years that they have ever been short-tempered with me. My brother doesn't remember the incident, and I have never asked the other two people in the car about it.

During those teen years, the aliens did a lot of reproductive procedures and tests. To a teenage girl who had never been to a gynecologist, the procedures were horrible. I don't know if I will ever be able to talk about it. After that last experience, I don't remember anything until I was 36 years old.

36-39 Years-old: They came back the summer of 1994. The first thing I remember was waking up one night, and seeing some of the mean gray ones standing on the side of the bed by my husband. I started screaming when I saw them. My husband awoke terrified because I was screaming about something on the side of the bed. As soon as I started screaming they went away. My husband doesn't have any memory of this. He doesn't even remember waking up and talking to me.

Not long after that, I woke up to find things moved around in my room. At that time, neither my husband nor I were sleeping very well. We were always tired in the middle of the day. My husband said he thought someone was touching him during the night. One night I awoke to find one of them in the bed with us. When she saw that I was awake, she sat up and floated off the bed. She continued to float about two feet off the floor at the end of the bed. I got up out of bed and walked toward her. I looked down between her legs to see if she was male or female. I saw nothing there, so I thought it must be a woman. She was only about 4 feet tall, a thin body with skinny arms and legs, very white skin, and long white hair. She had large eyes, and a thin line for a mouth, like the others.

What I thought was odd was the glow that surrounded her. It was an iridescent, whitish glow. It looked as if the glowing light was holding her up and helping her to float around. When I asked her what she was doing with my husband, she said she was just checking him out. She said that they approved of him and liked him for me. When she started talking (telepathically), I immediately knew her. A feeling of homesickness came over me. It was the same feeling I had when I was a child looking at the night sky and wanting to go home. As she held me, I cried and asked her to take me back with her. She held me for awhile longer until I calmed down a bit. She told me that it would not be much longer before they came back for me.

The next day, I went to the book store to look for something related to what I had seen. My husband was convinced it was a ghost, but I knew it was not. I knew that if I found a book with a description of her, then I could show it to my husband. I looked at the books on ghosts and angels, and could not find anything like her. As I was walking out of the store, the clerk asked me what I was looking for and if she could help me. Not wanting to tell her, I just said I wanted something interesting to read. She pointed out a book that had just come in to the store. The book was *Abduction: Human Encounters With Aliens* by Dr. John Mack. I thanked her, looked at the book, and said, "Yes, I will take it because I have always had an interest in the alien abduction subject." I started reading it the next night. In the book, I found a couple of references to a woman alien like the one I had seen. There were other references that were familiar to me as well. Finally I had proof that I was not the only one.

In the back of the book was an address to request more information. I wrote to the address and asked if they could refer me to a therapist. I knew I needed help and wanted someone that was open-minded to my situation. They did send me a list of therapists who were willing to work with abduction experiencers. I called and made an appointment with a therapist that was the closest to me. It took me a while to trust her and to relax with her. I wanted to get to know her method of therapy first. I did not want anyone that would make suggestions or lead me on, through hypnosis. The first thing we worked on was learning to relax. After learning to relax, I was able to talk about my experiences. After one of the sessions, I was upset and confused. It is a 2-1/2 hour drive from the therapist's office, to my home. The relaxation sessions seem to open up the memory, and I was replaying my memories over and over again in my head. One minute I thought I was losing my mind and the next minute I was okay with everything.

When I arrived home, I was still in a state of confusion. I knew what was happening to me but still did not want to accept it. A couple of nights after that session, I had a visit from them. I was sitting on a table and had my legs hanging over the side. Z (Z is what I call my alien counselor because his name starts with a Z) was standing in front of me, holding my hands, turning my arms around. He asked me why I had scratches on my arms. I explained to him that I had a new kitten in the house, that she liked to play a lot, and had sharp claws. He seemed perplexed about this. He then told me to lie back on the table and watch while he showed me something. There was a huge screen in front of me. I looked to the side and around me before looking at the screen. There were other tables next to me that were empty. The area was like an alcove off a hallway. One of the other aliens walked in front of the screen and Z told them to please use the hallway. No one seemed to be interested in what we were doing. Z showed me where I came from and where I was going to go one day. He explained everything to me. Afterwards he told me why I could never tell anyone about this. He said there were people here on Earth that would harm me to get the information he gave me. It was for my own safety that I not say anything. The love I felt for them was so strong that I could never betray their trust. After that visit with Z, I was able to start coming to terms with who I am.

There were other experiences after that. I will list them as I remember them: I remember waking up my husband and telling him to come with me because I wanted to show him they were real. This time they did not send anyone for me. They just told me to walk into the beam of light and I would be taken up to the ship. I told my husband to hold onto me and we would go up into the light. The light is an iridescent green color with sparkles in it. As we were going up, he hit his head on the ceiling. I could not imagine what could be wrong. The next instant I saw one of the aliens next to the light in our bedroom. He told me I could not bring my husband this time. I was upset and told them I wanted to bring him. They said there would be another time. My husband went back to bed. I went up in the beam of light. When I got there I was in a waiting room with other people. They were in their pajamas just as I was. While waiting there, a female alien came into the room. She was young and giggling. She was carrying a clipboard made out of clear material. She said she was not supposed to be in here but she wanted to come in and see what we looked like. She quickly left the room. Another alien then came in and walked over to me. He said he was taking me to training. We went to the engineering area for training. I was told we have everything stored in our memory, and that all they have to do is show us once how to do something, then when it's needed later, the memory is triggered. After the training I was sent back to my bed. I awoke to find the gray ones on the side of the bed. They are the mean ones that I do not like. I tried hitting one of them and heard a shrill high pitched sound. Then one of the white ones appeared on the other side of the bed, and told them to leave me alone, and that he would take care of me. The white ones are much nicer than the gray ones.

The next time they sent two white ones for me. There was one on each side of me holding my arms. Their touch was so light that I felt no pressure from their hands. As they were walking me through the ship, I asked them if they had come for me, to take me away with them. They said, "No, not now." I asked when, and I thought they said "45 years". I was upset and told them I did not want to wait 45 years for them to take me home. They had no idea that I had misunderstood them. Then I thought they said it would be the year 2045, and I was even more upset. They just shook their heads and said, "No, it will be 4 to 5 years." By then we had gotten to the area where Z was waiting, and he then explained a few more things to me.

After that time, the next visit was for a physical. It did not take long. It was like an x-ray that lights up your whole body. They told me that if I lay still, they would let me walk around the ship until it was time for them to take me home. After the test, I did walk around, but got into a bit of trouble. I was walking down a curved hallway. To my right there was a door to a room. I thought there was someone in there that was in trouble. I walked up to the door and the door opened. There a woman was lying on a bed, and an alien woman was standing on the other side of the bed, holding a baby. The woman that was on the bed, sat up when she saw me, and propped herself up on her left elbow. She had long, black hair that went down to her waist. When she sat up her hair fell over her right shoulder in front of her. She was not very coherent when she spoke, but she asked if I would please help her, because they were going to take her baby. The alien woman behind her looked frightened and held the baby close to her. I told the woman I would take her out of there and she could go home with me. She said no, because she did not want to leave her baby. I told her that

I would go outside of the room, and not let the alien nurse leave with her baby, and I would not let anyone into the room.

As I stepped outside the door, one of the mean gray ones was coming toward me from the right. To my left, I could see an alien nurse running down the hall toward me. The gray one wanted to hurt me to get me out of the way. Then one of the white aliens came forward and told the gray one not to do anything to me. He was going to talk to me, and everything would be okay. The gray one did not want to leave until this was resolved. The white one talked to me and explained what was going on. I then said okay and let them into the room. The nurse left with the baby. Then I went to the woman and told her what they said to me, and why they had to take her baby. She started sobbing and I was holding her, trying to comfort her. I told her to come with me, and I would take her out of there. She said she could not leave yet, because she had to wait at least another hour before she could walk. The aliens told me they would take her home, so I went back to the waiting room until it was time for me to go home. I would love to find out who that woman was, so I could reach out to her. Maybe I could explain a few more things to her, so that she would not feel so bad about them taking her baby.

There have been other times when I knew they had come for me during the night, but I had only fragments of memory about it. There are morning-after symptoms I get following a visit with them. One morning, as soon as I awoke, I was frantic and crying. I walked into the bathroom, and asked my husband to check my throat because it hurt so much. He said it just looked a little red. I knew that something had happened during the night. They put something in my throat, like an inoculation. Other times, I start getting very sleepy early in the evening, around eight o'clock. I feel like I have taken a very strong sleeping pill and I just can't keep my eyes open no matter what I do. I will go to bed and wake up 8 or 9 hours later still feeling very tired, as if I had not slept at all. This will happen three or four nights in a row, and I know they have been around. Other times, I will get the jitters or "heebie jeebies", as I call them. I know they have been here, or they are near by.

This is a situation that myself and other people have been born into. It isn't something I chose for myself. This was chosen for me. The love I feel for them is the same as the love I feel for my family. The love I feel for my family is for my relatives. The difference with them is that I feel a great deal of love for their whole race, not just the ones I know personally. They are an incredible race. While my eyes see them as strange looking, my heart sees them as beautiful. Some nights, I will look up at the star-filled night and hope that tonight I will see them. Each morning, when I let my cats in, I go out to the patio and look up hoping to see something. At times my heart aches with loneliness for them. It is difficult being a part of them and not being able to live with them. They are in my thoughts every day even if it is only for a few seconds.

This chapter cannot be ended without saying thank you to my husband. He has been, and continues to be my strength in life. I now know why we were brought together. The first time I laid eyes on him, I knew we would be together for a very long time. What I didn't realize at the time was how supportive of me he would be. After what he learned about me I thought he would head for the hills to get away, but instead he has done his best to understand what is happening. He would like to help more but doesn't know how. I tell him that letting me work through this on my own and listening when I talk about it is so important to me. His non-judgmental attitude and love is what I want and need. Again, I would like to say thank you to my sugarplum, my husband, my soul mate.

Note from Constance:

When I asked Kay about the symbols she used to begin and end her story, she told me that she had drawn them all her life, though she didn't know what they meant. Imagine my surprise when, fifteen months later, while attending a lecture by Scott Mandelker Ph.D., author of *From Elsewhere: Being ET In America*, I realized that he had drawn the same two symbols on the visual aid he used during his presentation. I later called Dr. Mandelker and asked him to clarify the meaning of these symbols. He said, that if considered from the perspective of sacred geometry, the upward pointing triangle indicates a transformation into higher energy, the self moving toward spirit. As it contains the spark of divine light, it can be understood as spirit in matter. The downward pointing triangle can be seen as spirit moving down into matter, thus implying a grounding effect. He said that when it follows something in writing that is positive, it's like a benediction, an amen, a "so be it".

I came across a letter Kay sent me in August, 1995 in which she described a dream she'd had a few days earlier. I included the letter so you can compare the details of her experience, first remembered as a dream, with those that emerged fourteen months later through hypnosis.

❖   ❖   ❖

Dear Constance,

I wanted to write and tell you about an interesting dream I had Saturday night. Rafael and I, and his nephew, were staying at a hotel for a weekend getaway. I went to bed about midnight. (Also, I had been very tired for the past couple of days, and I had slept for two hours Saturday afternoon.) I was still very tired so I went to sleep quickly. I dreamed I was in a hospital walking down a hall. There was a door open to one of the rooms. I walked toward that room to see someone. When I walked in, there was a woman lying on the bed. She wasn't wearing any clothes. All she had was a sheet draped over her middle. She had just had a baby, and the nurse was holding the baby on the side of the bed behind her. The woman looked all drugged up. She was worried about something. I asked her what was wrong, and she told me someone was going to come and take her baby from her. She was pleading with me not to let them take the baby. I told her I would go and get someone to help us, like the police. When I stepped out of the room, I closed the door behind me. There was a skinny man walking toward me and he was smiling. He was going toward the door so I held onto the handle of the door and wouldn't let him in. He just laughed, and said it was okay for him to go in. I started screaming and no one would help me. There were people at the end of the hall but no one would come. I wouldn't let go of the door handle. Next, a little man came to help the skinny one. He told the skinny one to shoot me. I looked at the skinny man, and saw he had a little gun, about 4" long, in his hand, and I thought a little gun like that wouldn't hurt. But then I remembered that it could hurt me if it was close enough to my body. I didn't want to get hurt, but I couldn't let them into the room to take her baby. I decided to pull a fire alarm, that was on the wall, and that would bring someone to help. I thought if I did it quickly enough they wouldn't have time to get into the room. When I pulled the alarm, someone came walking down the hall to see what was wrong. When I told her what was wrong, she just scrunched up her face and ignored me. I then returned to the room. The woman was still there, but the baby was gone. She told me they had taken her baby. She still looked doped up. I held her, and told her I would get her out of here, bring her to my apartment, and would take care of her. She said it was too soon to move, and she wanted to go back to her apartment. She said to come back for her later.

17

I don't remember anything after that. When I woke up I told Rafael about it. He asked me if I can remember who the woman was. She did seem familiar to me, but I don't remember who it was.

Oh, another thing about this weekend. Sunday morning we went downstairs to meet, for breakfast, with some people we know, who were staying there also. It is a couple that works with Rafael. The woman said she didn't sleep too well that night. I asked her why, and she said she was hearing things on the roof during the night. Their room was on the 9th floor which is the last floor beneath the roof. I told her it was probably the air conditioning units, because sometimes they are on the roofs of large buildings. I couldn't tell her what I was really thinking. I know Rafael was thinking the same as I was because I could see it in his face. Later he said there was no way they could come for me at the hotel. I think they can come for you anywhere.

Well, I have to close for now.
Thanks,

Kay

Note from Constance:

Sixteen months after writing her initial story, Kay began keeping a log of her experiences.

Kay's Update:

In the past, I have not wanted to write the experiences as they happen. Today, I have decided to start a journal of everything that happens to me, no matter how insignificant it may seem at the time. Fear has been the key factor in my not writing about the experiences, fear of people finding out, and using the information against me. Being involved in the writing of this book has given me a sense of duty to those who think there is no help out there. These people must be told they are not alone. My dear friend, Lydia, whose story you will read next, once told me she felt like a giraffe in a herd of zebras. When we met, she said she was happy to find out there were other giraffes in the world. It is time for us to come out from under the bed covers as I call it. My journal starts here.

April 3, 1997

Early this morning, something happened that bothered me because I don't think it was a dream. I awoke to the telephone ringing.

There was a girl on the phone. She said, "Hi, I just wanted to talk." I then asked her what time it was. She said, "Four thirty in the morning." Then she apologized for waking me. I told her that was okay, because I had told her to call me whenever she needed to talk about "them". It seemed like I knew her, like she was from some group I belonged to. She then asked if I would come over and talk to her. I said, "Yes, no problem." The next thing I know I'm sitting in a room with her. She looks to be about twelve or thirteen years old. She is very tiny with long, light blonde hair. The way she talked and acted was a lot older than a twelve-year-old girl should talk. We talked awhile. Then she looked out the window and saw someone coming. I assumed they were her parents. She said that she was glad they were here to meet her. I walked out of the window, and toward the people. There was a woman who was surprised to see me. She said she was happy that I was here and helping. I think she hugged me, but I'm not sure. When I woke up, my first thought was, I wasn't sure this was a dream. My second thought was, I wonder who that girl was. My next thought was that I had to call Lydia when I got home from work.

I called Lydia and told her about my dream. She said she had a dream this week about talking to a girl about twelve years old with long, white hair.

June 25, 1997

Scarlet, my cat, was walking around the house looking for a place to hide. I found her in my dresser drawer again. She is a very sensitive cat so she can sense when "they" are coming before I can. She does this hiding bit every time we get a visit.

Rafael lost one hour of time driving home from a business dinner tonight. After dinner one of his co-workers asked him for a ride home. The time was 9:50 p.m. when he dropped off his co-worker at his home. It takes about thirty minutes to drive from his co-workers house to our house. When he arrived he noticed the clock read 11:30 and he does not remember the drive home.

June 27, 1997

The time was 1:00 a.m. Rafael was crying in his sleep. I woke up when I heard his moaning and crying. As I tried to wake him up, he was saying, "No, no, leave me alone. Leave me alone." He then said, "They are trying to take X's and O's from me. I asked him what X's and O's he was talking about. He said they were on a tray, the X's and O's. He got out of bed and went to the bathroom. When he was back in bed, I tried to get him to talk. He said he did not want to remember.

He told me to tell them to leave him alone. The next day he was able to remember some of the experience. I was relieved that he was able to remember because it will help him to talk about it.

September 21, 1997

I remember floating up over my bed. I was face down, and as I was being lifted up I could see the bed below me. I was only about two feet over the bed. I was resisting, thinking about not wanting to go with them tonight. I was tired and wanted to go back to sleep, but they had other plans for me. It took a couple of more tries before I finally went. The last thing I remember seeing was the foot of the bed, and then I went up through the closet. For some reason unknown to me, they sure do like transporting through closets.

November 1, 1997

The instant I woke up this morning, I had a memory about something the aliens told me. They said that everything we see or hear is stored in our brain. This starts from the minute we are born, and continues until we die. Even when we are sleeping our brain is recording every sound we hear. We are not able to access this information as readily as they can, but one day we will be evolved to the point of being able to do this. This design of storing information in our memory was given to us as a tool for survival.

November 17, 1997

This morning I noticed blood blisters in my ears. The one in the right ear went away after two days. The one in the left ear lasted a couple more days. When I touched the area, it did not hurt or feel sensitive. My husband has had these many times in the past, but this is the first time I have noticed them on myself.

Note from Constance:

Working with Kay throughout these past three and a half years has been a joy. From a therapeutic perspective, she has experienced significant relief from her depression and anxiety. No longer feeling so different from others, her self esteem has improved greatly and she reports having a lot more energy. She has been able to resume working and is performing very well in her full time job.

During the past two years Kay has faithfully attended our group, but has seen me for only a few individual sessions, seldom requesting a hypnotic regression. It seems she is able to remember enough of her experiences consciously to live with them as they occur, leaving her free to focus on more mundane concerns during her sessions with me. For the most part, Kay seems reconciled to her dual reality, and she appears to be functioning quite well in both dimensions.

As for Rafael, his level of stress seems to be rising. He still chooses not to explore his strange experiences though they do bother him. I had the opportunity to interview Rafael in November of 1997 and projecting my own fear onto him, I asked him if he was afraid of being taken. His answer surprised me as he explained that he was afraid of not being taken. Suddenly I understood. What Rafael dreads more than anything else is that his beloved wife, the source of meaning in his life, will be taken and he will be left here without her.

On a lighter note, Kay once told me that as a child she dreamed of becoming an astronaut. When she told her parents, they said that would not be possible because she was a girl. They gave the same response when she later announced that she wanted to be a pilot, and discouraged her once again when she asked if she could join the Air Force. Kay said that after that she gave up on wanting to be anything. I find it gratifying that in exploring Kay's encounters through hypnosis, it has become clear that one of the functions she is being prepared for is that of flight engineer of the ship. And as for her present job on earth, naturally, she deals with aircraft.

As far as I'm concerned, Kay is a very good human to know. Not only is she delightful to be around, possessing a beautiful spirit and an open mind, but if ever the time comes that humans are being rescued from the planet and Kay is involved, I've asked her to stop by for me, and tell them...I'll do windows.

Chapter Two

Do You Know Where Your Children Are?

Prologue to Lydia's Story

Two months after beginning my work with Kay, Lydia called for an appointment. The path Lydia took to find me was just as amazing as Kay's. She had gotten my name from Dr. David Jacobs, the author of *Secret Life*. Dr. Jacobs, an associate professor of history at Temple University, had been a speaker at an abduction conference I had attended in Atlanta, for mental health professionals interested in doing this work. I later discovered that the sponsoring group, P.E.E.R., had compiled a Therapist Referral Network, and that my name was on the list.

Lydia presented as a lively, but anxious, married woman in her mid-twenties. Her husband worked as a laboratory technician, while Lydia stayed at home with their two small sons, one of whom she was still nursing. She obviously adored her children, relating that she and her husband hoped to have more. Lydia impressed me as an extremely kind and patient person, with a bright and curious mind. I was shocked as she began to relate the years of torment she had endured as a result of what she had finally identified as alien abduction.

I was able to see Lydia for a total of 20 hours, over a five-month period before her husband accepted a job which necessitated their moving to another state. Lydia proved to be an exceptional hypnotic subject, and it was my impression that therapy was extremely helpful to her.

In addition to their individual sessions with me, I asked Kay and Lydia if they would like to speak with one another. Both were driving several hours to get to my office, while they lived within 100 miles of each other. They agreed and soon were talking on the telephone. Before they met in person, each woman was able to give an accurate description of what the other had looked like six years earlier, when they had apparently seen each other on board a ship. Eventually they concluded that they were on the same "route." Kay and Lydia included their husbands in some of their meetings, and being together seemed to have a healing effect on all four of them.

After Lydia moved out of state, she stayed in touch with Kay through telephone calls and letters. When Lydia learned we were writing this book, she offered to contribute her story. I am grateful that she did, because her story has deeply touched me. Not only do I admire the courage with which she has faced her experiences, but I find the candor with which she relates her story to be compelling.

Lydia's is a particularly sad story, as she not only has missing time, but she has missing children as well. Like many female abductees, Lydia's teenage years were fraught with reproductive procedures, missed periods, and lost pregnancies as a result of her abductions. She was frequently in trouble for wandering outside late at night. Though her mother thought she was sneaking out, Lydia had no memory of leaving the house. Later, her lost children were shown to her during encounters, and when her first born son was four years-old, he spontaneously drew pictures of them.

The first picture was of a female with long hair, who he said was his sister. He had drawn a tear in her eye, and he explained that she was crying because she missed him. He said the second picture was of his brother. When Lydia asked him if he meant his brother, Joseph, his only sibling at the time, he became upset and said, "No, my other brother!"

For 16 years, I facilitated a support group for parents who had lost babies through miscarriage, stillbirth, or newborn death. Though I consider myself an expert in understanding the grief process surrounding the loss of a child, I can't begin to imagine what it would be like to become pregnant, despite using birth control, or in some cases, not having had intercourse at all, and then to have the fetus inexplicably disappear, only later to be shown a child and told it is yours. Worse yet, the people having these experiences have no books to read on the subject and no support group where they can tell their stories. Unfortunately, such has been Lydia's experience.

Lydia's Account: Written December 1996

I'd like to start my story be telling you how I discovered I was an abductee. It was 1987, and I was 19 years old. I was grocery shopping, and when I passed the book section, a book titled

Communion, by Whitley Strieber, grabbed my attention. I was drawn to it. I just couldn't take my eyes off of it. On the cover of this book was an image I couldn't ignore. I was mesmerized by it. It was a face that had haunted me for the past five years.

When I picked up the book, I expected to read about a ghost or an evil spirit. Instead, what I read was something from out of this world. It told of alien abductions. That was furthest from my wildest dreams, yet I knew that I had seen those enormous black eyes, that egg shaped head, the nothing of a nose, once before.

I wanted to get that book home as soon as possible. I had to read it. I hoped that it would shed some light on the thing I had seen in my room five years earlier. You see, the image of the being on the cover of that book was a mystery to me, one that I had needed to solve since the night it woke me up from a deep sleep. Here's how it happened:

I was fourteen years old when I saw the being in my room. Although looking back at my childhood, it's possible that I had seen them before. I had started dreaming of 'grasshopper people' when I was seven, and at age eight, I vaguely remembered playing with 'little blue naked boys'. One day after playing with them in the alley, I discovered a crescent shaped section of skin missing on the inside of my leg beneath my knee. My mother took me to the doctor who said he had never seen anything like it. The cut was too precise and there was no blood. It's interesting to note that my mother later told me that she dreamed of space men and that my uncle lived in a "haunted" house.

On the night in question, I was sleeping in my room when I woke up suddenly. I was aware that someone else was in my room. My heart began racing! I was very scared! My room smelled awful, I thought the house was on fire! I turned over and looked up. I saw this person in my room. All he was wearing was an old fashioned hat and coat. He had shoulder length, straw-like hair, huge piercing eyes, and an ominous presence. I exclaimed, "Oh, Jesus!" and then as suddenly as I had awakened, I was asleep again. I say that because that's all I can remember.

When I got up the next morning, I was very upset. I didn't know what to think or what to do. I got dressed, went into the kitchen where my family was about to have breakfast, and I joined them. Let me tell you, it was very hard to just sit there. I knew that I couldn't deal with this by myself. So, I told them about what had happened to me the night before.

My sister didn't believe me because she hadn't seen or heard anything. Her room was next to mine and the walls are paper thin. So she thought I was making it all up. My step-father had no comment, but God bless my Mom, she said she could tell something had happened because I was so upset. She asked me some questions, then told me that to her, it sounded like I had been visited by an evil spirit or ghost.

Well, I didn't want to be visited again, so I refused to sleep in that room. I told my mom that I'd sleep anywhere but in there. My mom didn't blame me, but since that wasn't a practical solution to my problem, she said that she would go into my room before bedtime and pray for God to bless and protect me from that thing. That gave me a little comfort, enough that I agreed to sleep in that room.

The ghostly image of that being stayed with me for the next few years, I would even dream of him or others like him. We would go places and do things. So you cannot imagine the feelings that came over me when I saw the cover on that book. For years I had wondered about that night, and the bizarre dreams I had because of it. When I began reading the book, I was shocked to find that it was devoted entirely to people who had seen the same beings.

I had an open mind about the book. It was interesting to see what other people had to say about those beings. I was totally shocked, though, by what I read. Only because what they said they had experienced was identical to the dreams and flashbacks I had been having.

I not only felt that what was written was true, I knew it had also been happening to me. It was as if the author of the book had interviewed me, and had written down my dreams and memories. And the more I read, the more I became convinced of this. The author wrote of strange experiments, of probes and implants being placed in the body. He wrote of missing time. All these things had happened to me.

But one thing he told of shook me to the core. Strieber told of missing or disappearing pregnancies. I had one just two years earlier when I was just seventeen. I had known I was pregnant. For three months I had danced around with joy because I was having a baby. My boyfriend was sure I had cheated on him because we always used a condom. But I didn't cheat, and I was pregnant.

Then one day it was gone. I went to the emergency room with my boyfriend, Brian, and the doctors couldn't find any evidence of the baby. There had been a lot of blood but there was no fetus. It was just gone. A three and one-half month fetus just disappeared. I was very confused and let down, but in a way relieved that I wouldn't have to marry a guy who didn't trust me anymore.

In this book, Strieber wrote of many things, but a lot of things had been purposely left out. I guess he did that so that when people wrote to him he could discern between genuine and fake accounts of abduction.

After reading the book, my whole life seemed to fall to pieces. I told my mom about the book. I told her that an alien being was what I had seen in my room that night. I said that lots of other people had seen and experienced what I had, too. She just kind of looked at me and said, "Honey, are you feeling okay?" She said she thought I should go see a mental health professional.

The idea of my mom thinking I was crazy, scared me. I was so afraid and worried, about being experimented on by aliens, and here she was saying I was just imagining it. Well, I'm sure hundreds of other people aren't just imaging it either. I knew I had to find a safe place to live, though at that time, I didn't know there wasn't one.

I had been living with my real dad. He had been out of town for three weeks and was due back in one week. I knew my mom would tell him I was crazy and he'd put me in a mental hospital, so I left. I moved out and into an apartment of my own. I wouldn't tell anyone where I was. I thought that would keep the aliens from finding me. I began sleeping in the day. I didn't think they'd come for me in broad daylight. Boy, was I wrong.

I stopped working, and lived on some savings I had. I stopped seeing my old friends and made new ones. These new friends believed my story. They even gave me some drugs to help me relax. I began turning to the drugs to help me relax, and to help escape my mind, and the memories of aliens. I kept using the drugs more and more until they made me so sick I nearly died. I even wished that I had. I didn't want to live if it meant I would be subjected to these ever-present beings in my life.

Where I lived, not much was ever heard of UFOs and nothing of gray, bald, black-eyed creatures, so most people thought I was crazy. To protect myself, I quit talking about it. I told myself I must be crazy, or that I had just been dreaming. But dreams don't leave bruises and scratches, or blood on pillows, or take away time.

27

So for the next six years I lived a lie, and told myself those things didn't, and weren't happening. I stopped believing myself, even though I still had many dreams and flashbacks. I would see images in my mind, of things that had happened.

When I was twenty-five, I thought that I had successfully gotten over that crazy period in my life. I had two children, a nice house, a loving family, only now my oldest child was reporting strange events. When he was two, he woke up one night crying and screaming. When I got to him, he said that monsters had come through his window, and had touched and poked him. He said that they pushed something up his nose. They scared him, and then they left. The strange and frightening part was, that there was blood on his pillow, and the next morning his nose was a little swollen.

Then more things began happening. Things I couldn't and wouldn't ignore. For example, one night, these beings brought a little girl to me, and said she was mine. Another night, a female being woke me up by jumping up and down on my bed. One morning, later, I woke up with what looked like hand prints on my arm and I recalled two beings trying to get me to go with them. Hence, the bruises on my arm from their three fingers and thumb.

I felt I was being slowly driven crazy. I couldn't stand it any more. These incidents drove me from my husband. I left him, took my kids and went to visit my sister. But there, I was awakened one morning by the sound of her moaning. Then for some reason, I looked out my bedroom window just in time to see a gray creature running into the woods behind her house. He was bluish gray. He seemed to be skipping or lightly running into the woods. He turned, saw me looking at him, and then seemed to smile at me. Well, I just laid down and went back to sleep. I wanted so badly to tell my sister, Judy, about it, but that kind of talk was forbidden in her house. Later though, when we were at my mom's, I told her what I had seen. I didn't care at this point if they did think I was losing it. I knew what I knew, end of story.

I went on a journey after that. I desperately wanted help, and I began searching for information on abductions. I thought, "OK. I have memories of these events". I planned to read some more books on the subject, then if they matched, I'd go from there. So, I read another book, but it didn't tell me anything new or different. There were still things that had happened to me that weren't written about, so it left some doubt in my mind. I wanted to know one way or the other if this was really happening to me, I felt I should talk to a trained therapist.

I decided I would read one more book. I chose *Secret Life,* by David Jacobs. Half way through it, I became discouraged and set the book down. Something made me decide to pick it back up, and read one more chapter. Thank God I did, because there was the description I had been searching for. Other people had been in a pool! Dr. Jacobs also described the mind scanning procedure I had endured.

I felt now that I wasn't alone, and I wasn't crazy. This book even gave an address to write to for help. Man was I relieved, I felt such gratitude. So, I wrote to Dr. Jacobs and told him my story. He then sent me the addresses and numbers of several therapists equipped to deal with my problem. I called the person on the list that was closest to me and, thankfully, that person was Constance. She unlocked the memories in my mind through hypnosis, and what they revealed to me was a lifetime of personal involvement on a scale I couldn't have even dreamed of. Under hypnosis, what had seemed devious, maniacal and life-threatening, now seemed loving, caring, thought provoking and a relationship of mutual caring.

I now have an understanding of these events in my life. I know that even though it's a little nerve wracking at times, it's something I've agreed to do. I may not like what they do, but at least now I understand it better.

Note from Constance:

In addition to Lydia's narrative account of her experiences, I am including the drawings she produced shortly after one of her hypnotic regressions with me. These images of her lost children were connected to her experience with a pool of liquid.

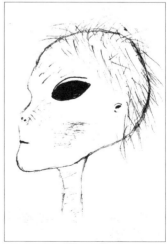

Figure 1   *Figure 2*

Toward the end of her therapy, Lydia produced this drawing of a female being with whom she feels closely connected. She describes her as "beautiful and so serene."

Figure 3

In August 1995, Lydia awoke from a nightmare. She was compelled to get out of bed and draw these pictures. She said she cried the whole time she was drawing.

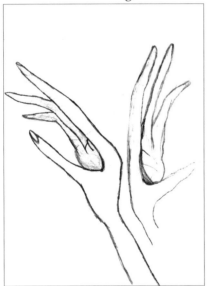

Figure 4

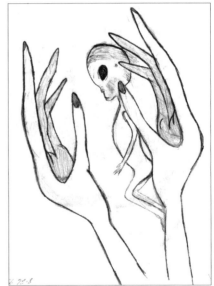

Figure 5

As you can see, the reaching hands that Lydia drew that night inspired the cover for this book. The idea for this originated when I showed the group Lydia's picture for the first time. I'll never forget the looks on their faces as Kay, Theresa, Robert, Daniel, and Sara stared at those hands. Later each described having a visceral reaction to seeing them. Finally, Robert said, "That's the cover of the book, and the title is _Reaching for Reality_."

Note from Constance: July, 1997

Lydia's alien visitations did not decrease after she moved away in August 1996. She kept in touch with me by telephone and I knew she had given birth to a third son. Having enjoyed nursing him peacefully for several months, she suddenly became inconsolably depressed in the spring of 1997. She decided to seek therapy and eventually, she found a hypnotherapist who helped her discover the source of her grief. Lydia flew down to join the group for a weekend in the summer of 1997, at which time, she wrote an update to her story.

Lydia's Update: Written July 13, 1997

As for the physical aspects of my recent abductions, I have had many medical procedures performed on me, such as tissue biopsies in my throat, on my vagina and close to my anus. Then there are puncture marks and later rashes appear that not even my doctor can diagnose.

The most disturbing procedure was during my third pregnancy in the eighth month. I had been sleeping on my back. I woke up thinking is that you (meaning the being). He said, "Yes, don't look." I was petrified. So to calm me down, he diverted my attention onto a piece of furniture. It worked. He then approached me and told me that they wanted my baby to be a certain way. And he gave me a shot in the stomach. Later I woke up on the other side of the bed on my side. Now I know that during the end of my pregnancies I can't move in bed without waking up, so it's a mystery how I got on the other side of the bed.

Under hypnosis, I discovered the source of a recent case of depression. It was so severe, all I can say about it was that it was a black period in my life. For three months I had grieved some loss, but I couldn't figure it out. Then I discovered that the being who had been with me all my life had died. Suddenly, I had a new guy coming for me. He told me Z had died, and that he would now take over.

He then took me to the ship, and began showing me its capabilities. He showed me how they drive, and how they stay in formation with other ships. Then he took me to the center of the ship.

While there, we met the oldest of my hybrid children. He tried to present me to the newest addition of this space family, but I resisted, not wanting to acknowledge its presence until several flying objects that I believe were operated by their minds hit me from all directions. The morning after this I was bruised from head to toe. At that time I couldn't imagine how it happened; after the session, I understood.

Note from Constance:

Not only had Lydia lost the being with whom she felt a loving connection, but the new guy coming for her insulted her intelligence with comments such as "You are really home in bed" and "This is not really happening." The last time I spoke with Lydia, she told me she was tired, that she just wanted to be left alone. She said she felt like she had done enough. I imagine that knowing her children are involved makes it that much worse.

I finally had a chance to talk with Lydia's husband, George, in November, 1997. I asked him what he found to be most difficult about his experience.

He said it was the sense of being helpless. "You don't know what the heck's happening. There are strange smells in the house. Sometimes you hear things in the night, but you can't seem to wake up. You feel that something or someone is in the house." He said one night he felt them grab his feet and begin pulling him off the bed.

George went on to say, "Your children tell you stories and they draw strange pictures." Recently he had awakened to find that his middle son had a scoop mark on his cheek. "You have a sense of failure, like you're not protecting your family very well," he continued. "You move a lot and try to hide in a crowd. I wish they'd take me and leave my family alone."

When I asked him if he had a history of abduction, George said he had always believed in aliens and been curious about the subject. He said he thought he'd seen a flying saucer when he was twelve or thirteen. He added that he had several phobias including a fear of small places and a fear of crowds. He added he felt like he had to keep moving and that he rarely slept more than five hours a night.

When I asked George, if given the choice, would he rather know what was happening to him, or not. He said, "I'd rather have my memories." He explained that, "It plays tricks on your mind. You want to know the truth." He said that his repressed memories had lead to depression and suicidal feelings. George said the worst part of the whole thing was that he couldn't answer Lydia's questions.

My heart goes out to Lydia, her husband and sons. How many more families like theirs are out there living through this nightmare alone?

Chapter Three

Thou Shalt Obey

Prologue to Daniel's Story

Daniel was the third of the seven to arrive at my office. Since I don't advertise my services, I'm always interested to know how people hear about me. This particular referral originated in Alabama when a bellhop suggested that I take a limo to the airport instead of waiting for the shuttle. I jumped in to find Anne and Whitley Strieber in the back seat. Whitley Strieber is a prolific author with world-wide recognition who, with the help of his wife Anne, has written about his abduction experiences. It was his book, *Communion*, that Lydia had found in the grocery store. I had read several of Whitley's books and had attended a conference in Alabama so I could hear him speak. I remember that Whitley discussed baseball with the driver all the way to the airport, and I kept thinking, "This guy has no idea who he's driving." Anyway, it turned out that the Striebers had moved back to San Antonio and were living within a short distance of me. Over the six hours it took for us to fly home, we became well acquainted.

Two months later, Whitley gave a speech in San Antonio. The Mind Science Foundation, which sponsored the talk, set out copies of an article I had written, titled "Are We Being Visited"? In the article, I announced a public meeting to discuss the UFO phenomena. Daniel, and his wife, Sara, attended Whitley's speech that night, picked up my article, and came to the meeting a month later.

It turned out that Daniel had been looking for a therapist who could help him deal with what he suspected were UFO encounters. Daniel had sought therapy for depression and was taking Prozac. Although the medication provided some relief, he continued to avoid going to sleep at night, feeling that he must guard the house. The resulting sleep deprivation was wreaking havoc in his life and he eventually found himself crying over TV commercials. He had been looking for a therapist trained in hypnosis who was open-minded on the subject of UFOs, and thanks to that chain of events, there I was.

Daniel was forty years old when I met him. A computer programmer with a B.S. degree, he was tired of his chosen profession and had gone back to college to complete the education necessary to become a high school math teacher. His wife, Sara, taught special education. Daniel and Sara had been married twenty-one years and it was obvious that their relationship was one based on devotion. I always have a good feeling in their presence, probably because they are so respectful of one another.

As of this writing, I have seen Daniel for seven hypnotic regressions over a two-year period. Sara joined for the initial appointment, but stated that she was not interested in undergoing hypnosis. She was there to support her husband, and when Daniel returned three days later for his first regression, Sara waited downstairs.

Following each of his sessions, Daniel went home and wrote what he recalled under hypnosis. His accounts represent an accurate description of what he related to me during those sessions. His accounts have been included unedited. The first two were written before I started the support group. The third account was written soon after Daniel and Sara attended the first group session. Since then, he has returned for more regressions and his narrative accounts of those sessions are included as well. Sara eventually wrote her account which appears as Chapter Seven.

Daniel's Account: Written February 1997

I write science-fiction as an avocation, someday as a career if chance wills it. As a result, the idea of encountering alien life isn't terribly upsetting—when considered in the light of day. In a Universe as large as ours, what surprises me is not that there is other life out there, but that we're not already up to our earlobes in them. Since life occurred once, it must have occurred many, many times and those who claim otherwise are both arrogant and engaging in pure sophistry.

We all spent a significant time of our childhood convincing ourselves that there is no bogeyman in the closet. Under attack by our parents and our more worldly peers, the Easter Bunny, Santa Claus and the bogeyman went down to defeat at the hands of simple logic. The world is a safe, secure place, a warm, cozy home in which to raise children and live out our lives.

Then, some of us discover to our horror that **there are bogeymen**. They have large heads, black teardrop-shaped eyes, gray skin and an unnatural interest in our biology. Like our childhood fears, they can walk through walls, make people freeze like statues and no one, not even our parents, can defend us from them. If ever there was something guaranteed to trigger animal fear in an adult, this is it.

In this day and age, it's almost impossible to be both conscious and unaware of the abduction phenomenon. Nearly all have seen a drawing of the bogeyman, or read one of the many books detailing our encounters with them. The likelihood of uncontaminated accounts of abductions is vanishingly small. We're involved in something strange and we want, no - we need, to know more about what's going on.

The bogeyman has not been forthcoming, so we read. We discuss our experiences in groups, and we do our best to deal with the fear. Most all accounts of abductions describe intense fear, terror that is often allowed to rage unchecked in the paralyzed victim's mind while the bogeyman has his way with us. Yet, in our group, with a single exception, the focus seems not on the fear, but on the desire to know exactly what is taking place. Yes, we are afraid, but it's not the heart-pounding, adrenaline-dumping fear that one might expect. We cope. We sublimate. We sometimes try our best to ignore it.

In my case, that fear showed up in odd behavior and depression. My wife and her family have been abductees for many years, though they've only been aware of the circumstances for a few years. I've sat with them at the kitchen table and wondered at their stories as they began pulling details out of the mists of memory. These are people I love. The hint that they could be crazy was unthinkable. After all, they are remarkably well-balanced people in all other aspects of their lives. I avoided the thought that I was involved, principally because it was too easy to believe myself simply jealous and wishing to share this aspect of their lives as well. After all, what could a writer want more than actual experiences with aliens? Bluntly, my motives were suspect, even to myself, despite a number of odd memories that seemed tantalizingly strange.

As time went on, I began having trouble sleeping. Not the usual toss-n-turn sort of insomnia, but rather a general avoidance of sleeping. I would spend the late night/early morning hours reading or writing, anything to avoid going to bed.

I began fighting depression that continued to deepen no matter how much I tried to persuade myself that the feelings were groundless. Eventually, when I found myself weeping over a car commercial on TV, I realized that I was unable to battle it on my own. I was keenly aware that the depression was irrational. I sought treatment from a physician and ended up on Prozac. Fortunately, the medication helped lift the depression. Still, the late nights and avoidance of sleeping continued.

Finally, during a visit with my wife's parents, a reason, a chain of logic, occurred to me, one that explained much of what was going on in my head.

To assume that my in-laws and wife were crazy was unacceptable, so I had to assume what they were describing was in fact occurring. At some level, I must have believed all along. Some creatures were taking my wife away from me on a fairly regular basis and there was nothing I could do about it. My anger, and my fear had to derive from worry that they might not return my wife some day. This explained the late night vigils. I was trying to guard my beloved wife. Everything seemed to point in that direction, and like a science fiction story, once you accept one fundamental implausibility the remainder of the story becomes plausible. Perhaps there was something to the odd little bits of memory I had been ignoring.

And so began my efforts with Constance, to try to determine what was actually going on. "Curiosity killed the cat; satisfaction brought it back." This may be a nursery rhyme, but it is also an accurate comment about human nature. In the short run, our curiosity can be very dangerous, if not lethal. But, in the long run, as a race, our curiosity got us stone tools, copper, bronze, iron, steel, the Industrial Revolution, and footprints on the moon.

Perhaps the strangest aspect of my experiences and those of the others in our group is a tendency to experience something bizarre, followed by an utter lack of curiosity about what happened. A mother and her two daughters are stopped by a UFO on a country road, and nothing is said about it for nearly fifteen years. My wife and I nearly collide with a UFO sitting in the middle of that same road, and we don't discuss it, or even remember more than a snippet of the event for much the same length of time. The first sign of an abductee is, in my opinion, a bizarre event utterly ignored.

As humans, we are both irresistibly attracted, and instinctively repelled, by the abduction phenomenon. If I could, I'd bring these assaults to an abrupt end with a bullet right between those depthless eyes. How dare these creatures treat us with such cavalier disrespect! Yet, the urge to explore the experience, to establish a relationship, is overwhelming.

I cannot prove, objectively, that the events related here are grounded in reality. I've yet to retrieve a single ashtray or monogrammed towel from the intruder's starship. But I believe, and frankly, I don't care who else believes. The truth will come out some day, and in the meantime, I'm coping. I seem otherwise sane and harmless without even the slightest urge to shoot up a post office. So, belief simply doesn't matter. Accept these accounts or not. The story is ongoing.

First Regression: December 22, 1995

I don't know what might come of this, but there are answers here somewhere. I may not be able to satisfy the world, but I can satisfy myself.

Today was my first experience with hypnosis, and though what transpired bore no resemblance to what Hollywood portrays as hypnosis, I must conclude that the procedure had the desired results. Sara has suggested that I write down the events of today's session, both to help me remember what took place, and also to ferret out any other bits that might come to mind while writing. Not all of what I'm about to describe was discussed with Constance Clear, the therapist, though I will be making a copy of this available to her. The material I didn't discuss then, has emerged while considering the events themselves during the remainder of the day. I will likely mix in my conclusions and speculations as I write.

We began the session with some idle chat, discussing a little of writing and my work with my writer's group. Constance asked me what I expected of the coming session and I had to admit that I really had no idea what I should be expecting. I explained that I'm a person with an empirical nature. We verify that something is working via experimental evidence, yet, in the case of hypnosis, as the subject, I cannot obtain experimental evidence. I expected some *sensation* that I could put my finger on and state: This is what it feels like to be hypnotized, but at the same time, I know better.

Constance turned on a white noise machine to help cover extraneous sounds. Within a few moments, the sound disappeared into the background, and I didn't hear it again until she switched the machine off at the end of the session.

We began with what I tend to think of as "standard" relaxation techniques, letting the body go limp and working to isolate and relax various muscle groups. Very quickly I closed my eyes. Normally, when awake, keeping my eyes closed requires an effort. Until the end of the session, it did not. I tried to avoid focusing on anything of a specific nature, choosing to count to myself while listening to Constance's voice. I'd count into the thirties and start over again at one. At some point after I *thought* I had myself quite relaxed, my right shoulder abruptly relaxed. Soon, while I still felt I could have simply stood up and walked away, I also knew that doing so would require a definite act of will. There was a sense of lassitude, a sense that I could move if I wanted to, but why?

Constance began talking to me about my "safe" place. I, at first, thought of the underground lab that often appears in my "sleeping" fantasies (the mini stories I tell myself when trying to put myself to sleep) but quickly switched to the concrete dome house I've often wanted to build. When Constance encouraged me to talk, at first speaking took considerable effort. I could offer only short sentences and single words. As the session proceeded, I grew more able to speak in greater detail. Why this is so, I do not know, only that speaking required an effort that I wasn't prepared to invest at first.

I described the concrete house, a concrete dome, circular, with a central access shaft for an elevator and piping. Constance asked me where my favorite place in this house could be found. I immediately flashed to the library, occupying fully a quarter of the dome's space, with many book shelves and books, as well as a comfortable La-Z-Boy. She asked me what the library represented. I responded, "reality." When she suggested that I envision my experiences as being on the pages of a book, I objected because that seemed to be making the events fiction. The idea made me uncomfortable. As an afterthought, my feeling that the library was the repository of reality strikes me as interesting. I clearly put great store in the printed word...not surprising given my writing.

Constance left that topic and we moved on to events in my childhood that might have seemed strange or unusual. I first started considering the butt slapping incident, and soon ... I should say here that there was no sense of "being" anywhere other than where I was, but instead more a sense of studying images, or catching fleeting thoughts and impressions as they occurred to me. I had, in considering this session ahead of time, determined that I would simply try to mention what came to mind without first examining it for some sense or order. Still, as I describe this, it will be useful, or simply more convenient to describe what I recalled as if I were re-experiencing the events. That may be the case, but the *feel* was quite different.

But, I digress...

I soon had an image of wooden, vertical bars, with rectangular cross section, like that you would see on a baby crib. There was a strong sense of being in a very, very large room. At first, Constance thought I might mean large with respect to a child's size, but the feeling was more of being in a dark, enormous hangar or other building. All was dark, except for my immediate surroundings, primarily those bars. I was young, about ten years old, and lying partially on my stomach, on my right side with my left leg drawn up. The pillow was thin, like a feather pillow, and had a plastic/slick cover on it. I could sense it "crinkling" with my movement. I later (after the session) got the impression that the mattress was quite thin as well, thin enough that I was gripping the edge of the mattress, though I described at the time gripping the blanket and sucking my thumb. My feet were bare, but I was wearing pajamas.

Constance asked me if I could move. I took a fair amount of time to answer that, considering it, and eventually concluded that I *could* move but would rather not. When she asked why, I answered that if I was still, I would not attract *their* attention. I couldn't supply any more than "them." When Constance asked if I could get out of the crib; again, after some thought, I decided that I could not, that the bars were too high for me. Constance asked if I could turn over to see what was behind me, and I told her that it would simply be the bedroom wall, but the impression was that I'd really rather not see what was behind me. The feeling may have been connected to my unwillingness to attract attention by moving.

At various times during the session, I grew aware of moving my head around, as if craning to see something, or straining to hear, or even simple puzzlement. For the most part, I was otherwise motionless, save an occasional twitch of a finger.

I told Constance that I could hear footsteps in the distance. In response to her queries, I added that they seemed from leather soles, and the steps of adults. There was a group of people making the sounds, more than a few. I had the impression of purposeful movement, as of people going about important work, and the sounds of office machinery, keyboards, and typewriters. At one point, I said something about lousy key touch, as if reminded of some terminal I've used in the past with miserable feel to the keys. Where that came from, I have no idea... unless I've used those keyboards?

I could see...or rather sense, the presence of a black, smooth, shiny floor, laid out in squares, like tiles, with brushed aluminum trim where the caulking would be in bathroom tile. While I couldn't *see* the floor, I knew it was there. Past that, I could not see. I have later added an image of a bright red ball, about two inches in diameter, attached to the bars of the crib in some fashion...just out of reach.

Constance asked how I felt about being there. Again, after some thought, I concluded that I really didn't care. It was as though I'd been there many times, and there was nothing unusual about the situation. I did feel a little insulted that I was sleeping in a crib, as I was too old a boy to be in a crib. The most overriding sensation was of being within a very large, mostly empty room. Toward the end of the session (I kept coming back to that empty room), I had the impression of someone standing near the foot of the bed, someone wearing a gray striped business suit. The image only shows me the sleeve/cuff of the suit, no hand or other detail. This image didn't solidify until after the session, while we were driving home.

Constance then asked me, "What happens next?" And I had no answer. When I considered the question, there was simply nothing there. I felt as though I were looking through a doorway with nothing beyond it...foggy, dark, vague, but in essence, nothing. The first time Constance asked the question, I felt somewhat frustrated by the lack of finding anything there, but not upset. At various times in the remainder of the session we returned to the idea of "What happens next" and each time we did, I became progressively more disturbed by the idea. At one point, I considered getting up and leaving, though I doubt if I could have done so. I told Constance that I didn't like this, and mused about what might be frightening me. Eventually, the idea became quite distressing and we moved on. I can't describe the feeling as fear, more that I simply did not want to be investigating past that doorway. I did not want to be *there*.

Constance then directed my attention back to the butt slap incident. I seemed to be in the same crib, but much younger, three or four years of age. Someone's cold hand slapped me on the rump, against bare skin. I described the slap as playful, stinging. I also described being dressed in pajamas again, this time with integral feet, footies, if you will. I described getting out of bed and toddling out to the living room to find my mother and father sitting together on a couch, watching Bonanza on the TV, in the fireplace. (That's where we had the TV in those days. My father built a wooden table/stand for it, a sort of primitive entertainment center.) I was upset, but not old enough to formulate any more than a demand to know why they woke me up. My parents insisted they didn't, and sent me back to bed.

I spent a fair amount of time trying to look around the living room of the old house in Fairborn. The only thing that seemed strange was the sofa on which my parents were seated. One, my parents didn't often sit together on the sofas we did have, and two, we never owned an over-stuffed black-leather sofa like the one I saw them sitting on. Constance asked if the room had a picture window, and I couldn't decide if that was the case or not.

I took us back to the large, empty room once again. I seemed drawn to that room each time we allowed another subject to relax. Again and again there was that sensation of "presence" of vast empty spaces, at the end, with rounded edges in the distance. The question of what would happen next still puzzled me.

About then Constance ended the hypnosis. My right hand had gone to sleep from dangling over the chair's arm, but I was otherwise in fine shape.

We discussed what had taken place, and I mentioned that there was something wrong with my ages in the various events. By age ten, we were living in the house at Lilac Hill, and by that time I had a "grown-up" bed and my bedroom was on the second floor. The bunk bed I recalled sleeping in at the time of the slapping incident was in the house on Arlington Drive, our first house when I was little. Constance speculated that I might be mixing two different events, and I agree. Given the sensation that I'd been in that empty room many times, I might very well have been mixing more than one event. I explained, that the "4th of July" dream didn't begin until we'd moved to Lilac Hill.

That ended our first session. If other details come to mind, I will add them to this file.

Some additional details have emerged. There is a large hatchway in the direction of my head, as I lay on my side. It is wider than it is tall, with rounded corners, and apparently provides an opening in a very thick bulkhead, twelve to fourteen inches thick.

There is someone standing near my legs, someone I cannot see, but the business suit seems connected in some way. And the sounds of workers in an office are coming to me from a point source near or behind the person standing nearby, as though the sounds are reaching me through another hatch or doorway.

Second Regression: April 8, 1996

We spoke for a while about hypnosis again, and the nature of reality. I described my latest set of strange experiences, i.e. awakening in the early hours of the morning to find myself very disoriented. In a couple instances, I thought I *should* be out in the living room on my La-Z-Boy recliner, even trying to lower the foot rest before realizing that I was actually in bed. The sense of disorientation is very strong, and rather unusual for me. At those times, I strongly felt that where I was awakening was not where I expected to awaken. It can take several minutes before I can properly identify the lights coming into the bedroom, and the shadows I should know well.

We started the session. I was focusing on a pen-ink drawing on Constance's office wall, that I suspect is Dr. Freud, before my eyes closed, but the after image suggested a face, and I tried to focus on that at the beginning. When she began to guide me in the direction of those nights when I awakened so disoriented, I jumped, startled. Something...or rather someone, was as startled as I. I'd awakened suddenly, in response to a touch on my shoulder, jumped and cried out in surprise, and he startled also, taking a short backward hop away from the side of the bed. It is a short, skinny fellow, with pale gray, almost white skin, a very thin neck with quite loose, wrinkled skin, like alligator skin, and a head which is too large in proportion to the neck. He wants me to get out of bed and follow him.

I am annoyed because, as I sit up in my waterbed, I reach for the cane I keep there, and he takes it away from me, setting it back against the bed stand where I keep it. My arthritis makes getting out of bed something of a challenge, and I use the cane to help me walk for those first few steps, until my back eases up. When I do get out of bed, it's much easier than I expect it to be. Constance asks me how I'm feeling, and I try to assess the sensations I'm feeling. The first thing that I noticed was that there was no pressure on the soles of my feet. I was clearly standing, but I could feel nothing under my feet, no carpet, no floor, no pressure, just a slightly cool sensation.

I heard a voice, which sounded like a person badly imitating a Texas accent. "You comin' 'r not?" The inflection in the voice, however, was not a question, more of an order. My impression was that the voice and accent were calculated to be calming, reassuring. The fella turned his back to me, and started out of the bedroom without a backward glance. He knew, without question, that I would follow.

With no transition, I am standing in the center of another area, again a very, very large open area. I'd estimate the room as over a hundred yards in diameter. I initially described it as too large for me to consider walking across without some effort. The ceiling overhead was a flattened dome, with eight curving arch supports of some tubular metal, with paisley-like curves inside the primary structure. The effect was beautiful, but also very functional. I could see that the curves were designed to aid in supporting the weight of the roof/ceiling. In the center was a cylindrical post-like thing into which the eight supports connected. The cylinder was translucent, and giving off light.

The perimeter of this room is lit with golden lights that seem to back light rows of instrument consoles of some kind against the wall. The lighting is soft, and reaches only part way up the walls. There are other people there, but I have the feeling that they have other duties besides worrying about me, i.e. they are otherwise occupied. I'm looking around this huge room, and the feeling I get is that I'm not supposed to be gawking about. The little man who brought me is walking away, again without looking, knowing that I will follow.

I notice that his butt is skinny as heck, and he has no apparent shoulder blades. He looks like what a child, given Playdough, would produce if told to model a skinny man...all smooth curves with no real joints.

Again, with no transition, meaning I don't remember walking across the floor or entering a room, I find myself in a darkened area containing a dentist's chair, thickly upholstered with arm rests, and a head rest already adjusted for the curve in my spine. The thing rests on a base that resembles the base of a standard, Stanton style, chess piece. The base is made of a metal which is gun-metal blue, but more shiny, more silvery. The upholstery is brown.

I climb up into the chair, and the guy disappears out of sight behind me. Constance asks about the surrounding area. The room is not as large as the domed area, but I cannot see past about three feet into the darkness. The area is lit, but I see no light sources.

Constance wants to know what the man is doing. I can't tell, but I feel waves and waves of frustration and/or anger. It's as if I were feeling his emotions like feedback squeal from speakers. Whatever is happening, it's not proceeding as it should, and that is frustrating the man. I'd *like* to move around, but I have the feeling that trying to do so would bring punishment, and I have the memory of an electric shock across the backs of my hands.

I become aware that I must be naked. I can feel the material of the upholstery on my bare back. It is like a big-pored Naugahyde, but doesn't feel sticky like Naugahyde does, nor does it feel like any kind of cloth. Somewhere along the way, my t-shirt and shorts have disappeared.

The level of frustration I feel from the man behind me is rising, and I feel as though I am only a part of the problem, that I'm more alert than I'm supposed to be, but there is also something else going wrong.

After what seems like a long time, two more men enter the room, passing on either side of me to join the original man. They move quickly, ignoring me. The original man immediately calms down. Constance wants to know if there's anything else I can see, or if I can tell what they are doing. I know there is an instrument console of some kind behind me, but that's from experience on another occasion, not because I can see it now. This console is like a raised pedestal, with displays of some sort, positioned so they cannot be seen from the chair. Light from the displays illuminate the face of the person standing behind the console.

Again, after a seemingly long time, I force down the footrest and stand up. I think I was ordered to stand, and I've been sitting in the chair long enough that I'm stiff from the lack of motion. By this time, I'm somewhat annoyed by the delay. They know I'm stiff and in pain, but that seems unimportant to them. Pretty soon, it seems unimportant to me.

Constance wants to know what happens next. I keep looking around, but it's as if someone hit FREEZE on the VCR, nothing is moving and there's no sense of moving time.

Abruptly, one of the men appears standing before me. He's shorter than I. His head comes only to about my chin level. He jumps up, and pops me one on the forehead with a rod-like thing in his hand, dropping back down to floor level. I jerk in surprise. The rod-like thing looks like a translucent Lucite rod. The end is spherical, and larger in diameter than the body. There is some illumination coming from the handpiece, and the inside of the rod has many silver sparks of light. I get the impression the tap was a warning, like we would tap a cat on the forehead to keep it from jumping up on the table. There's no pain, just surprise. Once he's done that, he goes away again.

Suddenly I see a rectangular hatchway, taller than it is wide, wider at the bottom than at the top, with rounded corners. It separates a thick bulkhead, at least six or eight inches thick.

The threshold is raised from the floor slightly, and I have the same feeling about it that one might from an elevator door...one shouldn't step on the crack. The room beyond is darkened.

Constance wants to know what's in the room. I tell her that either I don't know, or don't *want* to know. Later, after the session, it dawns on me that I'm *expecting* to see Sara, my wife and that's why I don't want to look. This is making me uncomfortable, and Constance suggests we move on, or call it a day, but I keep trying to see into that room. Suddenly, I can see into the room. There is another dentist chair setup in there, seeming to hover in the darkness at some distance from me, maybe thirty or forty feet. There are three more Gray people, and someone lying in the chair. I know this person. It is a woman, a light-skinned black woman with short, 'fro-ed hair. She's slender. At first I'm pleased it's *not* Sara, then guilty because I know that what they do to me, they're going to do to her. I know this woman, and feel attracted to her. I can't see her very clearly. It's as if you were approaching your car in a parking lot. From a distance, you can't see the details, but you know what the details are and supply them mentally. She is, or seems to be, asleep in the chair, and she is naked as well.

At this point, Constance asks what it is that they do to us, since I mention that they're going to do the same thing to this other woman. I remember being poked in my back, two places above each shoulder blade, and there is coppery-searing pain for a few seconds. I remarked that the only upside to this is that you don't remember it afterward. I'm sorry they're going to do this, to this woman.

I feel like I'm pushing my luck in some fashion by looking through the doorway. I think it was being permitted grudgingly. Eventually, someone grabs me by the left wrist, forcefully enough to hurt a bit, and pulls me away from the door. I can feel his flesh on my wrist, and the sensation of three fingers and a thumb is quite clear. The digits are long enough to circle my wrist quite completely, and his touch is cold.

Briefly, I toy with the idea of shaking loose, and swearing at the man who's holding me, but make a conscious decision that it wouldn't be wise to do so. There's the distinct feeling that these people are not to be messed with, that punishment can be severe. On the other hand, I also have the feeling that this time, I'm being permitted far more latitude than usual. Why, I do not know. Maybe it has something to do with whatever went wrong with this visit. In thinking about it, I don't know if the threat of punishment is real, or if I've simply been made to believe it's real, as if they've decided that's the best way to handle my particular personality.

I'm being led back into the large, domed area, toward the center. Reaching the center, I'm trying to look around, and find myself standing on a square area laid in small, square tiles, like bathroom tile. There is a pattern in the tiles. The pattern is moving and shifting constantly, like large pixels on a computer screen.

Again, with no transition, I'm back in my bedroom. I can remember no details about getting back into bed, but I am certain this is the night I woke up thinking I *should* have awakened in my arm chair, out in the living room.

Constance brings me back out of this, and we discuss more of the details I can remember. I remark again on the sense of impending punishment if I fail to do as ordered, and my feeling that these people are not to be messed with—they *can* make one's life miserable if you don't obey. But that doesn't seem too upsetting. It's as if these are rules that I have accepted and agreed to follow. I mention again that I know the woman in the other dentists chair, but can't put a name to her. I hint that we've been intimate, i.e. that I've been intimate with the other woman. That's quite upsetting, because later, on the drive home, comes the nasty feeling that I've had sex with this woman at sometime. That is *very* upsetting.

Sara and I speculated a bit about why that might be. One possibility is that Sara is probably not fertile any more, but then, neither am I. It also occurs to me that this other person might really *be* Sara, but I want so much for it *not* to be that I'm supplying another woman in Sara's place. It also might be that the aliens are exploring human relationships, trying to see how the bonds between Sara, me and other humans are structured, maybe even interracial relationships. The upshot is there's no bloody telling what they might have in mind.

As I'm emerging from the "trance", I get to wondering why I can't remember these things normally. We discussed the theory that *everything* we experience is stored in memory, but that we retrieve memory via connected links, i.e. something reminds you of something else. Everything we remember is remembered in a context of some kind, what we were doing, or in relation to something else that leads us to the memory. That we can't remember these abduction experiences suggests one of two things. Either there is no context for these memories, i.e. we can't connect them to anything else that would let us get back to the memories, or something is breaking/weakening the context that would lead us to the memories.

This leads me to wonder if I can't set up, ahead of time, a "context" in which to store these memories and make them more accessible. Both sessions have started by following a fragment of memory, the awakening in the crib, and now awakening in bed feeling disoriented. If I could structure a waking memory ready to link to the events in the night, maybe I could then get back to the memories later.

Somehow, the subject of their appearance comes up. Their necks are really scrawny. I suspect I could easily snap a neck. The head isn't really over-large, but it seems large in proportion to that neck. The eyes are large, and black, with epicanthic folds like Asians that gives them a slant-eyed appearance. There is a nose, mouth, but the chin is receding to the point of non-existence and the nose and mouth are too small. There are small ears, set too low on the head.

On the drive home, I'm terribly distracted, trying to quickly tell Sara of all that happened. I manage to miss our turnoff, and we have to take the expressway loop around to get home. That night, I stayed up quite late, fiddling around to no profit, unwilling to go to bed.

It occurs to me, in reading back over these two sessions, that a constant theme is the sense of restriction I feel when in their presence. Don't move, don't argue, do what I'm told, all against the background of some kind of threat of punishment. Yet, at the same time, I'm at peace with that decision to obey. These are rules I have accepted, willingly, and will obey.

Third Regression: July 8, 1996

It has been the better part of a month since the session took place and I've been putting off writing this up. I haven't been able to decide why; the session has been on my mind the whole time. A part of what bothers me is that it seemed so utterly real, yet is exactly the kind of thing I would come up with for a story. It strikes me as odd that we came into the "story" in the middle, backed up to a "beginning" and then followed events to the end of the session.

49

Constance asked me to simply state what images I might be seeing as a means of starting the session. There was something involving my father, and then I found myself sitting on a bench with several other people in an enclosed space that I knew to be the inside of some kind of transport, like a truck or shuttle bus. Across from me are a middle-aged blond woman in a simple cotton summer dress, and a teenaged boy in a t-shirt and jeans. Their body language gives me the impression I'm looking at mother and son. Next to the woman is a tall, thin black man with short hair who's wearing jean-material overalls. On my left is an older man with graying hair wearing a business shirt and slacks. On my right is another woman, younger, with brown hair. She is clad in a jogging outfit, a red jogging outfit. We are all barefoot.

The floor of the shuttle is coated with rough, black friction tread material, like that you find on stair treads. The walls are smooth, white plastic, with storage areas overhead, so that we have to lean forward slightly on our benches. We entered via a ramp that forms the rear wall of the enclosure, to my right. I'm very incurious about my surroundings, as though they are familiar. I've seen these people before, but don't know their names, and don't think I've spoken to them to any great extent.

Constance asked me to describe what took place before we got into this shuttle. We walked there across a wide, concrete floor, in single file. The area is large, like an aircraft hanger, and dimly lit. As we approach the craft, I'm struck with its simple, clean lines, and a sense of pleasing functionality in its design. It's pleasant to look at, roughly rectangular with rounded edges, and slightly sloping sides. For some reason, I'm reminded of the Golden Ratio when looking at this vessel.

Again, Constance asks me to back up. I'm in a waiting room, like a jury waiting room, with a large group of other people, all sitting around on folding metal chairs, patiently waiting. The room is what you'd expect to see on a military installation, white-washed walls with green trim, and fluorescent lights hanging from the ceiling. From time to time, groups of people, scattered among the rest, simply stand up and leave; groups of six. There's no one giving us directions. Eventually my group's time to leave has come, and we walk to the shuttle.

Once aboard the shuttle, the ramp closes, silently. There is no sense of movement at all, no acceleration of any kind that I can feel. After a time, the ramp descends again, and we rise to leave. We step out onto a wide catwalk suspended in the midst of an enormous bay area, with hundreds of identical shuttles docked in rows next to ours. The place is so huge that details fade into the distance. We are one of several groups in the immediate area, walking down the center of this catwalk, again in single file. The surface is solid, like cast concrete, and though normally walking on something with no guard rails that high in the air would give me the willies, I don't seem concerned. There are levels similar to this one both above and below us. The place is busy, active. These people think, and build, BIG.

There are people standing at various intersections wearing brown uniforms. I'm not close enough to any of them to see any detail, or even tell if they are human. Before we get close enough to the nearest one, we turn at an intersection, and approach a dark opening.

There is a memory gap here, or I'm somehow "moved" to a new location. I'm alone, the rest of the group is gone. I'm also in total darkness, though I sense that I'm in a relatively small room. Suddenly I realize that I'm naked and that brings on a flash of outrage and annoyance. They do this to us, often without warning, and I think they do it purposely to put us off balance, make us feel vulnerable. I know that I'm being examined, though there's no sensation of being touched. The floor is cold, but the air temperature is comfortable. I have the impression this is a regularly scheduled checkup.

Again, the memory gap effect. I'm suddenly back aboard the shuttle, and I know we're returning. I'm with the same group of people. At this point, Constance brings the session to a close.

Reality is a relative thing. When I'm writing a story, I strive to make the story as real as possible in my mind, knowing that it's the little details that make a story come to life for the reader. I'm accustomed to "living", for brief times, in worlds that do not exist outside my own imagination. I've practiced developing images that are as real as I can make them, down to the texture of the surfaces and the smell of the air. It's when these imaginings are at their most real that my writing is at its best.

Yet, these experiences with Constance are equally as real, as solid. The *feel* is different. There's not the sense of hunting details for a story, to create veracity. Constance asks me to look around, and the details are simply *there* for me to see and feel. The whole sense of the process is different. Still, I wonder. I have quite the imagination.

Fourth Regression: October 8, 1996

The Learning Channel has spent the past week running shows about the UFO/Abduction phenomenon, working really hard to blame these things on RF-caused plasma balls near earthquake sites, and over-stimulated human temporal lobes or sleep paralysis. We discussed these theories, and the flaws contained in them, wondering why we haven't used RF generators to create our own plasma balls and/or detect earthquakes. Nor do they explain scoop marks on people's bodies or other reports that fall outside the norm. I expressed my worries that these theories seem to suggest that our minds are an imperfect, and unreliable instrument with which to judge reality. If we cannot trust our minds to place reality, what *can* we trust? I find that thought worrisome—very worrisome indeed. Reality isn't a point-source; it's a region.

Prior to the episodes with waking "in the wrong place", one of only two distinct memories of something unusual is one of encountering something on a dirt road in New Mexico, something in the road that I had to avoid. I remember seeing a landing strut support of some kind, and a vaguely cylindrical object, just after we rounded a bend in the road. I swerved to avoid the object, drove the Jeep we owned at the time, into the bar ditch, and kept on going. Sara was with me, but does not remember this incident.

This is what the session with Constance revealed about this memory.

Sara and I are driving in my CJ5 Jeep. We are late and, I am driving faster than usual. It is just after sunset. I told Constance that we were on the Mangus Turnpike, on the way to Sara's parent's house. More about that later.

It has gotten dark enough that all I can see is what the headlights reveal as we drive. We enter a bend in the road that has a curved, multi-layered shelf of shale on the outside of the bend. As we come out of the bend, I see the object. We are going to hit it. There's no time to react. I yank the steering wheel to the right, and it is turned under my grip even faster, as if the wheels had gripped, and jerked the steering wheel around on me. Somehow, we managed to avoid hitting the thing. For quite a while during the session I fixated on how we *should* have hit the object, but didn't.

Initially, I thought we hit the bar ditch and kept going, without commenting on what we saw. That would be unusual in itself. In that part of the country, if you encounter another car that's having trouble, you stop to help. As I tried to focus on what happened after we passed the object, I realized that I'd popped the clutch as part of the effort to stop and the engine stalled as we slid sideways in the dirt bar ditch, ending up on the far side of the ditch, stopped just at the point of hitting a large cactus or pinion tree.

The object was, in the glimpse I caught, roughly cylindrical, about the size of one of the butane tanks common in that area, large enough to reach from side to side on the road, about twenty feet. There are four landing struts, two at each end. They are quite robust bits of hardware, beefy and clearly intended to take considerable punishment. I think the Jeep's left wheels rolled over the disk-like foot of the near strut, as we passed it. The surface of the tank-like part of the object is white, but not smooth. It has a texture to it, like seams and welding marks...detail of some kind that I didn't see clearly.

I am quite frightened. My hands are shaking and I want a cigarette very badly. Initially, I tell Constance that I just sat waiting for the adrenaline charge to wear off, then got out, and paced next to the car while waiting for Sara, who'd apparently wandered off somewhere, leaving me with the impression that she would return soon. I recall hearing gravel crunching next to me. Still, all I can see is my hands on the steering wheel, and the vegetation in the headlights. I recall being concerned that the headlights were on, without the engine running. The more I considered the pacing, the more strange that felt, as though there were two people, one pacing, one sitting behind the wheel. The memory of pacing does not *feel* real. There is no detail to it, only the sound of gravel crunching under foot. Throughout this, I am quite anxious, frightened, well out of proportion to a near miss accident.

Quite suddenly, I felt a warm sensation on my left shoulder, as though someone had suddenly clapped a hand over my shoulder. There was a presence beside and slightly behind me; a presence that was not Sara. I do not turn to look, though I can clearly feel the three long, warm fingers and thumb on my shoulder. I flinch away from this thing, and want desperately to get away. I don't frighten easily, but I'm terrified of this thing, terrified enough to want to run and hide. But I don't move. I can't say if it's because I *can't* move or I simply *don't* move.

This seems to go on forever. Eventually, Sara returns, coming from the rear of the Jeep. She climbs in and buckles her seatbelt. I punch in the cigarette lighter, and start the Jeep, I am in a tearing big hurry to get out of there, and have a cigarette. I don't know where Sara's been, assuming that she'd gone to find a bush.

At about this point, Constance brought the session to a close. During the time when I reported being very frightened, I know I was moving around quite a bit on the chair. Even after Constance ended the session, and for a goodly portion of the trip home, I could feel those fingers, that hand, on my shoulder. When she "awakened" me, my heart rate was still slightly elevated.

On relating this to Sara, she reminded me, rightly, that at the time we owned the Jeep, Sara's Mom and Dad lived in California, not Mangus. Therefore, we probably weren't on the Mangus turnpike and definitely weren't on the way to their house. While she doesn't remember this event, she does remember being with me on a dirt road and being very anxious, without further detail. This leads us to wonder if the surrounding stuff about trying to call her parents, finding the phones out of order, and going there for dinner isn't part of a false memory laid in, to help cover what really did happen. I had considerable difficulty in arriving at the details I did, and these were surrounded with a considerable amount of fear. I cannot remember being that frightened at any "normal" time of my life. I even have to wonder if more than what I've described took place, or if I was simply being held while something was done to, or with Sara.

A couple days after our last group session, Sara came into my bedroom on the way to take a shower and found me sleeping on the right side of my waterbed, on top of the covers, something which is very unusual for me. I remember waking feeling like I'd been dumped onto the bed, but didn't make much of it, merely moving back to the "correct" side of the bed and going back to sleep. This might prove a useful thread for the next session.

Fifth Regression: March 19, 1997

My in-laws live in Wyoming and we often visit over various holidays; Christmas, Thanksgiving and the like. This last Thanksgiving we flew up there for a short visit. Sara's parents are also abductees, and our shared experiences are often the topic of dinner table conversation. We trade our latest experiences and latest speculation about what in the dickens might be going on. Sara has reported encounters in this house, and we've joked many times about the aliens following us across the country.

When we stay over at their home, I generally sleep on the hide-a-bed in the basement. The basement is finished, with a wood pellet stove for additional heat. The mechanism of the stove feeds a few pellets at a time to the fire, which causes the flame to dampen when the pellets first hit, then flare back up as the new pellets catch fire. This can make for ... interesting shadows in the otherwise darkened room.

Knowing this ahead of time, I always check out the room carefully from my position on the bed, to familiarize myself with the new shadows and shapes in the darkened room, just to help make sure I don't waken with a fright over something that's just a shadow. There is, for example, a La-Z-Boy type chair not far from the bed, with it's back toward the bed. I studied that for a while, to get used to the shape, which, with a fair amount of imagination, could be made into the shoulders and head of someone in the room.

While staying there, during the Thanksgiving holiday, I had three strange encounters, of which the following is one—I believe the first one. This is, of course, while under hypnosis with Constance guiding the session.

I awaken in the bed, lying on my side, facing the door, and the arm chair I described above. I can't see well—my glasses are perched on the arm of the sofa alongside me. There is someone standing behind the armchair, looking at me. I start, but look carefully, aware of how the chair might look in the shadows, but no, it is a little, short Gray, with extra long arms, longer than they would be if this were human. I remember seeing him appear. It was as if he stepped around an invisible corner, appearing from right to left as though being revealed by a sliding, invisible wall.

Quite clearly, I sense, "I'm not here—just roll over and go to sleep." I obediently roll over on the other side, but I'm wide awake with a strong urge to roll back and see what's going on. I just can't seem to summon the energy to roll over. The room is lighted, both by the fire and by light that I believe to be coming from a wide, ground-level window over my head. There is a bluish quality to the light. Soon, I'm feeling much more calm. I'm lighter in the bed, more comfortable and my hips, which always hurt in an unfamiliar bed, are not hurting. I usually sleep in a T-shirt and shorts, but suddenly I find myself wearing something with sleeves and cuffs, like cotton PJ's. Someone takes my clutch pillow away from me, gently tugging it away. I'm actually having to exert effort to stay asleep, as though I'm determined to get to sleep despite some annoyance that's keeping me awake. I am a little annoyed. I'm not in that bed any longer. I can't see anything, the area is utterly dark. There is a coolness to the room that wasn't there before, and the bed covers are gone. The surface is more uniform under me. I'm still on my side, curled up in a defensive, fetal position. It's getting cooler. Maybe if I stay asleep this will pass—play possum long enough and they'll leave me alone. I don't want to be here.

Someone has touched my shoulder. They are shaking me gently; it's almost a comforting, tentative, stroking touch. There is great power in those fingers, a gentle strength that I've felt before. The fingers urge..."you go." I roll over and straighten out. Now I can feel the surface I'm laying on, it is hard and smooth, yet I'm partially weightless. A Gray is standing alongside. He has enormous eyes, big God damned eyes. He bends over and gets right in my face. There's no detail in those eyes, no pupils, no texture-they're just empty. I'd like to move away; he's definitely in "my space," but I can't move. I can feel his breath on me, we're two inches apart, nose to nose. I want to avoid that gaze. He blinks once, slow unhurried. The eyelid is milky white, translucent. I can see a fine stubble of hair on his forehead. I think he shaves there.

He backs away and I can see the ceiling. I shouldn't be able to see this well. I can't feel my glasses on my nose; I assume I'm not wearing them. The ceiling's dimly lit and I can see machinery, but little in the way of details.

There are more people in the room now, at least three more. They are shorter, but the same general body style. They are simply standing, waiting for instructions from the tall one. I itch in several places, and I can see movement in the ceiling overhead—things moving in precise lines, machinery of some kind.

I don't know if they sat me up or I sat up. I think the tall one put his hand on my shoulder to help me sit up.

He's probing between my toes on my right foot, running his fingers between the toes, and it hurts. I'm a little embarrassed—they might not be as clean as I'd like. He's trying to feel the bone structure, pressing hard, and bending my foot around. This is one of the shorter ones. The taller one nods to him and he steps back. No one speaks. I'm still wearing these cotton trousers and light cotton shirt. The material is white. I wonder if they are making a concession to how uncomfortable being naked makes me. The trousers close with a simple drawstring.

56

The area is dimly lit, with overtones of beige. There is other equipment around. I feel like I'm expecting them to do something. There's a sense that something is about to take place.

A tingling sensation begins at my foot, then works its way up both legs toward my hips. It's like the limbs are going to sleep, or rather recovering from it, a reflex tingle. It's cooler than I'd like. My right arm is held out straight away from my body. Someone is holding my hand, bending the fingers back and forth, watching how the joints move with great intensity.

Constance is being very quiet this session, letting me go where the memories take me. That's making me a little uncomfortable, as though there's a finite amount of inertia in what I will remember, and I've used it up. I sense something like a flexible plastic sheet that I'm pressing up against. On the other side are memories, events that I can't quite get to. Either I don't want to reach those memories, or I'm being blocked from them.

I begin getting a series of rapid images. Very clear images, but of extremely short duration. Before I can describe each, I've moved on to the next one.

I've entered an auditorium. There are many people in it. I think most of them are Grays. The auditorium is semicircular; I've stepped in through doors at the back. The lighting is subdued, and the feel is of a social event. There are some humans down there—they stand out. One man is wearing a white T-shirt and jeans. He's about 30 feet away. He stops and is talking with someone, standing hipshot, relaxed. The seating is a series of benches that follow the contours of the room. Some Grays are seated. We're getting ready for a presentation. My feet are bare.

There is a keyboard I'm familiar with. A display console is above it, with numerous icons spread across the surface. Each is some variation on a fancy crescent moon with brilliant colors, reds, oranges, yellows. The colors seem to have to do with the level of urgency for each icon. The screen has fine, gold grid lines on it. Some of the icons are drifting slowly. Streams of data are going by inside an oval window on the console. The data is supplemental to other things on the display, details about things. I'm supposed to read everything that's in green characters and read the rest if I have time.

Another icon is yellow and resembles a hammer & sickle. My job is to make adjustments. If you touch one of the icons, it can be "dragged" along the console display. I've gotten good at it over the years; accustomed to how it works, but I can't tell you it's function.

Each succeeding image is of shorter duration.

There are some Grays on a platform, one with his hand up in the air, like a student raising his hand.

There is a slender black woman walking across a stage.

A dentist's chair with stands next to it, and tools attached to the stands.

I see Saturn, from not very far away.

I'm walking down a fairly steep ramp, trying to be careful where I step.

I'm sitting in a waiting room. There are three other people just waiting with me. There is a single bright spotlight on each one of us.

I'm following somebody down a hallway, again dressed in cotton PJ's. We're passing door-like openings with beige panels.

Constance brings the session to a close at this point. I'm a bit disappointed that the session disintegrated into such fragmented memories. There's no sense of closure, or completion to the memories, especially to the memory that started the whole thing.

In retrospect, though, there is the staring business. This is the first time I've mentioned it, though I've heard of other people describing it. The sensation was uncomfortable, but not repellent. What the fragmentary memories mean, I don't know. Each snatch seems unrelated to the others, but was absolutely clear and sharp in my memory.

Sixth Regression: May 22, 1997

I should note, at this point, that this hypnosis session took place long after I wrote the introduction to my experiences. Considered in that frame, the results of this session strike me as even more intriguing.

After the previous session, I found my confidence in the process to be quite shaken. It was easy to conclude that the fragmented nature of the last session was the result of my subconscious not having prepared a credible story to tell for the session. As I've said before, I still doubt myself in the face of an utter lack of physical evidence. Like the risk of tornadoes or cancer, that sort of disaster happens to other people, not me.

The results of this session were, however, radically different, and horribly revealing. Some elements of my character now have reasons behind them, events that explain my attitudes and behavior in some areas. In some ways, that's the most frightening aspect of this session.

As usual, Constance and I discussed a possible focus for the coming session. I mentioned a dream I have had on a fairly consistent basis since childhood—a dream I have labeled my "Fourth of July" dream. I cannot now say whether this dream actually came to me each 4th of July for a number of years, as I believed, or if it is a repressed memory that is triggered by watching fireworks on that holiday.

From about the age of ten, we lived in a colonial style mansion/house that was built during the 1800's in Ohio, just off a branch of the Ohio-Erie canal. In its day, it had been a hostel on the canal, and was built to face the canal, and a set of locks that no doubt also served as docks. Mansion may be too pretentious a word to describe this house, but it was huge, 70 feet long and some 50 feet wide, with two stories, 12 foot ceilings and five-course brick walls from the basement to the attic. When the house was built, the front (narrow) end had a formal porch, with Roman columns supporting an upper porch accessible through doors at the end of the upstairs hall. Today, the formal porch remains, but the upper porch has been removed and the doors replaced with a tall, wide window. My parents speculated that the change had been made to cure leakage problems in the porch roof. It had been possible to sit on the upper porch, and look out over the river valley below. Today, a grove of lilac trees would mostly obscure that view.

In the dream, I am a small child standing on that upper porch, having come out through the French doors, watching a display of lights in the sky. There are dozens of the lights, all brilliant, vibrant, almost-living colors coming from spherical objects that look smooth. They fly about in complex patterns that remind me, now, of the kind of patterns made by lasers in concerts, that depend upon persistence of vision to trace designs in the air.

Having discussed all this, we began the induction. Constance suggests I return to one of these dreams to see what really happened. I answer that something has awakened me, a small child of about ten. In my pj's, I walk down the upstairs hall, and come to the French doors that lead out onto the veranda. The doors are framed with sheer curtains, gathered with ties to hold them to the side. I push on through the doors, and go out onto the porch. There is gravel under my feet, which is a part of the conflicting experience—there is not now a porch there, the roof that is there now is covered with fine gravel and roofing tar.

At this point, something odd happens to my perspective on the events I'm reporting. I'm watching this small boy as he watches the lights. He's a tow-headed blond, standing on the porch with his head tilted back, mouth open in awe at the display. There is light everywhere and nowhere, with no discernible source. The lights are strong enough to be casting shadows, however. The spheres are dancing in the air; reds and blues and greens and violets, all brilliant, alive, fluorescent colors that seem more intense than I've ever seen before. The little boy is wide-eyed with amazement and delight.

Constance asks me how I'm feeling about the display and I respond that I'm pleased to be seeing this again, rather like getting to watch a favorite TV show. She asks me to return to the time before, when I saw these lights.

I pause, consider this, then, abruptly I'm standing on the porch to our house in Fairborn, seeing the wooden grape arbor that serves to make the walkway into a green tunnel to the front door. I'm standing in the dark, looking out through the squares of the trellis. I'm a little boy, less than seven years old. The colored lights are in the sky, there are several of an emerald green that I really find myself attracted to. There are no white lights. I'm dressed in footed pj's, the white ones with the mounted rodeo cowboys all over it. I tell Constance, in a small voice, that I'm going to get in trouble for being out on the porch at this hour. I hear myself answering Constance, speaking like a child, and yet the adult is still present, feeling a little sheepish at speaking childishly, yet exerting will to not interfere. It is, I must say, a most bizarre sensation.

I push open the front door, slowly, because it squeaks, so as not to wake anyone. The sensation of being two people, the child and the adult, grows stronger. I wake up out of a nightmare in my bunk bed, huddled up against the wall. "I woke up with a jerk," I said, and grinned, the adult in me seeing the joke the child made inadvertently. I'm scared. I tell Constance, still in that small voice, that I'm worried that I'm going to be found dead in the morning. Both the child and the adult know this is a silly fear. I need to go to the bathroom. The bunk bed I'm sleeping in has wide boards at the edge to keep me from falling out and it takes a little effort to climb out of the bed. The whole time, I'm keeping an eagle-eye on the folding closet doors in my bedroom. The doors are white pine with horizontal slats. I'm expecting something to come out of that closet.

I sneak past the closet and start down the main hallway. I stop at my rocking horse and suddenly experience a rush of emotion over finding the rocking horse. It is blue, with real leather reins and gold-colored scrollwork on the rockers. My grandfather made it for me and it must have meant a great deal to me. I began to tear up over the sense of loss of the rocking horse, while smiling and laughing with remembered delight. The child climbs up onto the rocking horse and begins to rock...rather determinedly, I think.

The front door is open and that startles me. It should not be open and there's a bright white light coming through the door, spilling around the edges. I'm not tall enough to reach the door knob, but I think that's an excuse. I'm still rocking, and really frightened. I'm still answering Constance in the child's voice, and still watching as an adult. "I'm gonna get in trouble—I'm not supposed to be up. I wonder if Daddy's outside."

I climb down off the rocking horse, and sneak toward the door. "I'm scared." I don't want to look around the door, and I can't get to my parent's bedroom without going past the door. The adult is amazed that this little boy could be this frightened, and still function, still move toward that door.

The light is bright, fluorescent, bluish. "I don't know what to do. If you run, they'll get you anyway. The monsters." The adult tells Constance that the monsters are bigger than me, with slender hands, arms with no joints, big heads and eyes like insects. They never say anything. Their touch is warm, sometimes it burns. The child is too frightened to speak.

I remember seeing the light before, coming from inside my closet, through the slatted doors. The child wonders where Lady is, our Collie. She should be up with me. The child is carrying his blanket, his thumb firmly stuck in his mouth, as he creeps toward the door. It's finally too much for him, and he sinks to his knees, then curls up tightly on the floor, his eyes screwed firmly shut. The adult has to back away. I'm too close to the terror this child is experiencing. I can feel his heart racing. He's breathing hard. His hands are shaking and he whimpers. He hears the screen door squeak as it opens, and curls up even tighter with a moan. Someone picks him up; I can feel the hands on my back and legs. They carry him. I'm crying again, and the terror

61

that boy felt is real, immediate, and there with me in Constance's office.

The hands are too warm, and soft without being hard. They don't feel right. The adult withdraws even more from the child, and some of the fear is gone. But the boy had his eyes closed—if he didn't see it, I can't describe it. They lay me down on a table, on my right side. The surface is cold and smooth. I hear something like a heart beat in the distance. Thump, thump, thump. Cool air is going by me like a fan. The adult recognizes the feel of air conditioning. My feet are cold. I'm naked, and I still need to go to the bathroom. I'm ashamed of being naked. There are hands on my knees—they want me to roll over. I just curl up tighter. "But he's really strong, and they'll hurt me if I don't do that. I just better do what I'm told."

He's standing over me; I opened my eyes. They all look the same. He knows I'm afraid, and tries to tell me it's not gonna hurt, but I know he's lying—it's gonna hurt. My stomach is mildly upset, real time. The lights are shining down on me from above—the lights from the dream. They're on the ceiling and they move around above me—the same brilliant, vibrant lights.   He's bending my arm at the elbow, over and over again. I jump because he tried to bend it backwards and it hurt. The adult backs off again as the little boy grows more frightened. The little boy is lying there on the shining metal table, his eyes wide open, and too scared to move. He's wet himself, and the monsters are taking samples of the urine. The adult cries out, "Leave him alone! You're scaring him!" I close my eyes. I can't believe I wet myself, and I'm embarrassed. Humiliated is the word the adult supplies. "I want to go home!" the boy whines.

I'm back in my bunk bed. I've wet my jammies, but I'm too tired, too frightened, too drained to go clean myself up. I'm crying, and just stick my head under the pillow, hoping it'll all have gone away in the morning. This child is terrified, desolate, and hopeless. There's nothing he can do to stop this, and Mom and Dad don't believe him when he tells them about the monsters in the closet. The sense of being alone and helpless is overwhelming, like being naked, and alone in the center of the Astrodome, in absolute darkness.

On the upside, I think the boy managed to pee all over the monster, and he takes a tiny amount of satisfaction in that.

Constance wakens me, and I come around still crying and trembling with rage. The first thing I said, "If I ever get my grubby paws on those gray bastards, they're dead meat." I hate them for frightening that child, that badly. If they're ever silly enough to let me loose, I will kill as many as I can get my hands on. I can still, even now, sitting at the keyboard, feel the fear that boy experienced, the heart-stopping, freezing terror he faced, utterly alone and helpless. There's no excuse, none, for causing that kind of terror in a person.

It takes a few minutes for me to recover. I believe the dream is the examination room sublimated into something less frightening, a source of wonder instead of terror. This is that little boy's attempt to defuse the fear he endured.

I described to Constance the strange feeling of being there as both the child, and the adult. I'm still uncertain of how to describe that, but the adult could draw back from the child at will, and needed to a couple of times as the fear grew too intense. At other times, the adult let the child speak, watching from above, and restraining the urge to supply vocabulary as the child spoke. Very, very strange sensation.

I've told Sara on several occasions, notably after that attack, a number of years ago, on a McDonald's in California, that the great sin there, was not that people were killed, but that they were made to be afraid, helpless. I know now why I'm personally so obsessed with being always prepared to defend myself, to never, ever let myself be caught that alone, that helpless, that afraid. And I know now, the source, of the cold, calculated, matter-of-fact determination, to kill any Gray I can get in my sights. They keep me immobilized because they know how dangerous I can be. I wonder if I can ever forgive what they did to that little boy.

Note from Constance: October 1997

In reading Daniel's account of this last session, it is apparent that he was confused by the appearance of himself as an adult interchanging places with the child reliving the experience. What he didn't recall is, that I had given him a suggestion that the adult he is now could go back and offer comfort, and support to the child he was then. I used this technique as a way for Daniel to distance from the intensity of his experience, and to mitigate the terrible loneliness the child had experienced. I had no idea how effective this technique would be in allowing him to access the emotions contained within that brave and terrified little boy. Daniel, the adult, could finally express the righteous anger that Daniel, the little boy, had never dared to acknowledge.

It was a psychotherapeutic breakthrough of vast magnitude. At last, Daniel understood why he had devoted so much of his energy to maintaining control over himself, and his environment. In this painful-to-witness session, Daniel lanced the boil at the core of his difficulties. He had faced the hardest of all human emotions...total helplessness.

Only Sara could tell us if he's easier to live with as a result of his work in therapy, but I can report that Daniel has completed his education, and achieved his dream of becoming a high school math teacher. From all appearances, the job agrees with him, and I hear that his students adore him. It might be that impish sparkle in his eyes.

Four months after this session, Daniel surprised the group by saying that he no longer felt homicidal toward the beings. Somehow in working through his feelings from his last session, he had come to realize that in spite of the terror, helplessness, and humiliation he had suffered, it was not the intention of these beings to hurt us. I noticed he wasn't carrying the concealed hand gun, that for years had been his constant companion.

Note from Constance: December 1997

As they say in my profession, progress is an illusion. Two months after I wrote the above conclusion to Daniel's chapter, he had an encounter that set him back.

Seventh Regression: December 2, 1997

These events apparently took place Thanksgiving night, 1997. I've seen Constance, and the following is the result of the session. Now, almost two weeks later, I strongly suspect I'm doing more traveling than sleeping, and I really don't want to record these events. I feel that I must, however, before I manage to rebury the memory.

For the first time, I am overtly frightened by what's happening to me. I've finally had evidence, that I cannot persuade my back brain is just a bug bite. I've known in an intellectual fashion that strange things are happening, and there's always been the sense that some of my experiences were unpleasant in the extreme — but now there is no avoiding that knowledge.

The morning after Thanksgiving, the both of us slept in, since we have no children, and no family were visiting. Sara joined me in bed, and happened to ask me if I'd been aware of the dogs' behavior during the night. The question itself brought on a feeling of unease, but aside from that, I remembered nothing unusual taking place during the night.

Sara then told me, that at about 3:30 the dogs, who sleep in Sara's bedroom, woke up, and charged out into the living room, barking excitedly. She got up, turned on the house lights, and investigated, but found no reason for the dogs' reaction. They calmed down, and in a few minutes Sara and the dogs returned to bed.

Around a half-hour later, the dogs repeated their performance. Both times Sara checked me, to see if I'd awakened, only to see me apparently sound asleep. She told me that each time she was tempted to come in and wake me, but thought better of it.

Frankly, I was still tired and half-asleep and didn't think too much about it, though it did seem strange that the dogs' barking didn't wake me. Under normal circumstances, it certainly would have.

That evening, while in the bathroom, I reached to scratch the nape of my neck, right at the hair line, just below the hollow of the base of my skull. I found a tiny bump that was just slightly tender. It had a scab that fell away at my touch. Nearby was a slightly larger bump.

A bit startled, I had Sara take a look. She reported an injection site, just like the ones you get from having a blood sample drawn. The second bump was not visible and was probably unrelated. A chill went through me, and my hands began to shake. Whatever this was, it was *not* a bug bite.

In general, I would have let this pass, waiting until our regular meeting to report it. I have found odd "bite" marks before. This time, however, was different. I had Sara take a number of photos (which we have not had developed yet), and I decided to call Constance. I told her what I've related above, and we agreed to a hypnosis session for the following Tuesday. During the conversation, she reported friends and neighbors having heard, Thanksgiving night, a thunder-like rumble sound in the area of Constance's neighborhood — a sound that lasted much longer than could be easily explained by lightning. In one case, the sound woke an entire family.

I found myself approaching the session with some trepidation, the same kind of distant fear which a person afraid of heights might experience while looking up at a high bridge. One comment that emerged during the pre-induction discussion was that I'd finally been confronted with something that the ape within me could not be convinced was just a bug bite. I had evidence the primitive part of my soul couldn't discount or twist into something normal. My intellect can deal with these events; my instincts cannot.

Thanksgiving evening had passed uneventfully. We had dinner out and I spent a quiet evening reading, something my job keeps me from more often than I'd like. I eventually fell asleep with the book in my hand, then woke up long enough to stow the book and turn out the light.

The induction went smoothly and Constance reviewed with me the events prior to going to sleep. I have arthritis, as I've mentioned before in these accounts, and I was apparently in some pain that night. I normally ignore the pain when talking to other people — they don't want to hear about it, and I'd just as soon forget it myself. That night I could not get comfortable, and spent some time trying to decide if it was worth getting up to take some codeine. I have, over the years, learned some pain management techniques, guided imagery, that sort of thing, to help me reduce my dependence on pain relievers. That night these techniques were not terribly effective, and I ended up tossing and turning, never quite getting up the will to go get the pills. Eventually, I managed to succumb to sleep.

When asked about anything unusual happening that night, I sensed two disturbances, as if there were something I should have remembered. I looked into the darkness of the night and found two — somethings — that I symbolized as dimly lit heaps, discontinuities in the uniform black. What I describe next, I'm virtually certain is entirely symbolic, a way of describing the indescribable.

I found myself walking down a dark country lane. The surface underfoot was hard, and rounded, like roads made to shed rain water. The dark is nearly impenetrable. I am comfortable, without pain, and seem relaxed. I can sense more than see the tree line to either side of me. As I walk, I encounter a huge, white rose glowing in the dark. The flower is large enough to cover the entire road, but it is not illuminating the surroundings. It is quite beautiful and I stand for a while in contemplation.

This, I'm sure, represents the first disturbance. I resume my walk, and, after a time, I encounter a second flower, equally as large, glowing in a slightly yellow shade, a carnation. This is the second disturbance, different in texture and substance from the first. Neither flower is visible from the other — this seems important.

Constance has me return to the rose and I see myself stepping through the petals to the center of the flower. The petals come to about knee-height.

Thou Shalt Obey

I cannot now relate the transition, but I am suddenly lying on my side on a polished steel table, my knees drawn up with my hands clasped together tightly between my thighs. I'm cold and clammy — I've been sweating. I'm being told to hold very, very still. The surface of the table is warm where I've been touching it, so I've been there for some time. I'm aware that I'm wearing boxer shorts. I *never* wear boxer shorts.

I'm trembling with fear and dread, terrified to move and desperately anxious for this to be over. Something cold touches the back of my neck, I quiver and am told again not to move. In my minds eye, I can see a tiny needle penetrate my skin and a glowing white thread, like fiber-optic cable, emerges from the needle, sliding down alongside my spinal cord. I flinch. The pain is horrific. It's as if every nerve in my body has suddenly swollen to the size of hot-dogs, pulsing and throbbing with white, coppery agony. I can see, as well as feel, the pain, like a glowing hot copper bar. It has a life of its own, a presence with suffocating mass, engulfing and overwhelming me in white-hot weight. My mouth is flooded with the taste of metal, strongest on both sides of the root of my tongue.

They tell me that the pain is my fault, that I moved. I beg, plead with them to make it stop. On the chair in Constance's office, I tense, locking up every muscle, twisting in the chair with the remembered agony. I'm aware of Constance's horrified reaction, aware that I am frightening her, but don't really care. I must describe these things, somehow rid myself of them in the telling.

At the height of the writhing, I arched my neck and opened my eyes, as I did during the procedure, and to reassure myself that I wasn't then actually experiencing the pain. I made a panicked visual sweep of the ceiling, a quick glance at Constance, just long enough to verify her presence, then closed my eyes again.

Constance said something, I don't remember what, and as suddenly as it began, it was over. Still sitting tense in the chair, I described the table and the mechanical waldo that operated the needle probe, declaring that the process was too delicate to trust to manual operation. I've seen this device before. It has a chromed-silver, conical shaped muzzle from which the needle and the glowing thread emerge. The fitting is knurled, as if it can be removed from the device by unscrewing it.

I tell Constance how terrifying the machine is and that I would kill to avoid the procedure. If I could, I would destroy any creature who tried to force me to endure that pain again.

Suddenly, in response to some words from Constance, I am walking behind a Gray, the first time I've seen one in this session. I'm close enough behind him that I can only see the back of his head and upper shoulders. I realize that I am not walking, but I am standing on an escalator and we are rising. I want very much to wring this bastard's neck, and tell Constance that it would snap off easily. Despite my desire to attack him, I make no hostile move.

We are in the mall-like area that I've only recently begun to recognize as a common feature of many of my dreams. The area is huge, the decor 1960's imagined 21st century, with lots of chrome, polished metal, plastic, transparent partitions and bright light. Most of this detail is supplied from memory, for on this occasion I can only see some twenty to thirty feet around me. We approach a platform that seems suspended in midair, though I know it leads off to my left, toward the examination rooms.

Once again I'm on that table, working to sit up. The edge of the table is slightly above the center, making it hard to get my legs swung over the edge. I'm sore all up and down my right side, the side I was laying on. As I look around, I seem to be in a doctor's office, but I'm perfectly aware that it's an illusion. There is ultramodern equipment mixed with antiques, including a battered white antique dry sink with a cabinet above that has rectangular glass panes set in chipped and cracked glazing.

As I sit up from the table, I experience another stab of pain, a vertical slice of muscle-cramp-like pain just to the left of my breast bone. This was both real-time and remembered pain. I clasped it with my right hand and moaned. In a few moments, the pain eased and I could relax some.

Constance, anxious I think, to get me away from that room, asks me about the shopping mall. I've been there many times, wandering about its vast expanses. There are all manner of different shops and I've spent many hours exploring them. There are other people around, people whom I know and some I've become friends with. Strangely, I don't know any of their names. We sometimes sit together in groups, in sunken conversation pits laughing and joking with each other. As a group, we're completely at ease with one another. The example I used for Constance was, that we could tease our Catholic members about being Catholic, and they laughed as hard as the rest of us did — in short, those things that we might normally be sensitive about were unimportant to us.

When we conclude the session, my hands are still shaking, and for a minute or two I'm quite disoriented, not quite sure of where I am. I know that we do not remember pain, only that pain was felt, yet I could still taste the fear, and pain of that examination.

Constance called Sara in to join us, while we discussed the session. As we talked, I absently scratched my left shin, and discovered a fresh scoop mark that had scabbed over from the previous night. It was about 3 mm in diameter and neatly circular. There was a short skin tag on one edge as if whatever scooped out the divot didn't quite cut perfectly cleanly at the end.

In following good writing practice, I've let the above account cool for a few days, then read it over again, patching a sentence here and there. Time is putting on some distance from the pain, but this still isn't comfortable to think about, let alone write about. Furthermore, if anything, most of this account is understated. I had about reached the conclusion that our little Gray buddies could be forgiven their deeds, and, given "cultural" differences I think it's wrong to ascribe either evil or malice to their actions, but that does very little to calm my anger and outrage. I'll get over it, but it still wouldn't be safe for the Grays to let me run loose aboard one of their ships.

Chapter Four

To Know or Not to Know?

Prologue to Theresa's Story

Sometimes I wonder which is better, knowing or not knowing? To acknowledge the reality of alien intervention in one's life, is to accept the isolation that goes with being fundamentally different from other people. So, I wrestle within myself regarding the advisability of using hypnosis to uncover buried experience. Rather than pretend to know what is best for my client, I have learned to follow Milton Erickson's lead in trusting my client's unconscious mind to make the right decision. By weaving in suggestions such as, "while your conscious mind may be curious about your experiences, your unconscious mind is willing and able to monitor the process, allowing you to remember that which is beneficial to your well being", etc., it is my intention to invite and respect the response of the unconscious.

In the case of Theresa, who had interviewed several people before coming to me for hypnosis, her unconscious mind said "no". Try as she might, Theresa was unable to penetrate her experiences through hypnosis. It wasn't that she didn't achieve an altered state or that she didn't receive additional information, it was just that each time an image emerged that wasn't part of her original conscious memory, her conscious mind surrounded it and picked it to death. This was agonizing to watch especially since this is pretty much the way my own conscious mind tends to act.

The other part of the story was that, unlike the others who had sought my help, Theresa was not experiencing any major psychological symptoms; no depression, no panic attacks, no low self esteem. Indeed, she was a happily married mother of a precocious four-year-old child working along with her husband to run a very successful family business in a small town. Theresa has studied linguistics and is fluent in five languages.

Theresa arrived in my office in the spring of 1996, four months after I had begun seeing Daniel. She had decided to seek help after her daughter, Alex, reported seeing a UFO hovering over their house. Initially, Theresa contacted a local UFO group and was referred to a UFO researcher. She decided not to see the researcher because the individual did not have credentials as a therapist. The researcher referred Theresa to a psychologist in a nearby town, who had an interest in working with abductees, but didn't do regressive hypnosis. The psychologist had met me through Whitley Strieber and when Theresa contacted her, she passed the referral on to me.

Theresa and her husband, Robert, made three trips to my office in hopes of utilizing hypnosis to uncover information regarding a series of bizarre experiences involving the two of them as well as their daughter.

Each time I took Theresa through a relaxation sequence, she became more and more tense until her eyes popped open. Ultimately, Theresa became so frustrated that she sought the help of a UFO researcher, who used some sort of contraption to get her into trance. Apparently, he was no more successful in helping her reach her goal than I had been. It was my impression that Theresa's unconscious mind was telling her to leave well enough alone. If it ain't broke, don't fix it! Or, as Carl Jung wrote, "The unconscious will have it's way".

When I started the group in July of 1996, I invited Theresa and Robert to attend, and throughout the past two years they have rarely missed a session. They are a delightful couple, both are extremely bright, articulate, athletically fit, and nice to look at. Robert is a gifted architectural engineer who is well read in science.

Theresa mentioned recently that she would like to try hypnosis again, and that she would like for me to use a more directive approach. The following is her story based on the facts as she consciously recalls them.

Theresa's Account: Written December 1996
Symphonies & Robberies

Hello. I'm pretty much the girl next door. I'm perhaps your neighbor or acquaintance you've met through business functions, church socials, or any other event that might take place in a small central Texas town where everybody knows everybody. My name is Theresa, I'm twenty-eight years old, happily married, and the mother of a five year old daughter, Alex. I think the town folk would view me as a nice girl, "from a really fine family". My husband, Robert, and I are both well educated and traveled. I was fortunate enough to begin my higher education in Europe. My husband is from central Europe, and the old world value system is very much at the core of his being. We own multiple businesses across the southwest. The blend of our educations and cultural backgrounds makes a valuable sounding board for the subject of extra-terrestrial relationships with human beings. Why am I telling you all this? Because it is important. Contrary to popular belief, alien abductions are not exclusive to the schizophrenic living on the streets of New York City. This phenomenon spans the social, economic, ethnic and global spectrum.

The realization of my involvement with alien beings has been a gradual process that is not yet complete. On one hand, I teeter on the edge of complete disbelief because, as we all know, "this can't possibly be happening". On the other hand, I am faced with the raw facts of memory fragments, unusual dreams, physical markings, and the testimony of my husband, my daughter, and my dear friend of personal encounters and sightings at our home. It is difficult for the conscious, intellectual mind to accept such a reality because relationships with extra-terrestrials are not a part of our collective knowledge as a society. In other words, it is not a part of our educational, political, religious, or family values. Another reason for the difficulty in full and conscious knowledge of extra-terrestrial relationships stems from the extra-terrestrials themselves. It is apparent from personal experience as well as from the accounts of thousands of abductees that clear and full conscious recollection of abductions are clouded by alien induced amnesia. I don't know why this is, but I must admit it makes very little sense. I find this the most frustrating aspect of the entire experience. So, bearing this in mind, I would like to tell you as much as I can remember, the menagerie of my experiences.

The first concrete experience I had began on the evening of July 5, 1993. Robert, Alex and I were organizing ourselves to leave for the Rocky Mountains where we own a business and a second home. Around dusk, I was in the kitchen packing travel snacks for the car when I suddenly had a very intense stinging pain in the small of my back. It was not a deep, muscular pain, it was definitely "skin pain". My immediate thought was that I had been stung by some kind of nasty insect, like a wasp, or even perhaps a scorpion. I frantically shucked off my clothes and yelled for Robert to come help me. I found nothing in my clothing, nor did I see any kind of insect fly away. Robert came to my rescue, examined my back, and found a "funny spot" on the center of my spine at the small of my back. As we examined it more closely, we discovered that the "funny spot" was actually a scab approximately the size of a dime. It was in the shape of a perfect circle, and within this circle were seven geometrically positioned punctures:

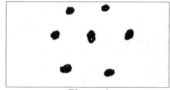

Figure 6

It was not a thick, crusty scab made of dried blood, instead, it seemed to be more like that of a burn, thin, rather soft, and somewhat opaque. I remember thinking that it looked like someone had "plugged" something into me. We just can't understand why I didn't feel this wound when it was inflicted. I have no recollection of an accident or injury to my lower back, nor did I engage in any unusual activity to cause such an injury. Two days prior to the incident, I had worn a new pair of denim shorts and thought perhaps there was a seam that might have irritated my skin. So, I tried the shorts on, but there was no such seam. Why would it just suddenly and intensely hurt like that after a scab had already formed? Why can't I remember how and when it happened? Why was the wound geometrically proportioned?

The next day, we left for our business trip. On the night of July 12, exactly one week after the mysterious "burn" on my lower back appeared, I had another unusual experience. I call it my holographic alien experience. We were still in the Rocky Mountains. Alex was asleep and Robert and I settled into bed around 11:00 p.m. and we both felt unsettled, or anxious—which is very unusual. Just as I was beginning to feel relaxed and sleepy, I had a very strong thought that said very clearly, "Go to the bathroom". I thought to myself, "That's silly, I don't feel that I need to use the restroom". But, again, the intrusive, clinical thought instructed, "We don't want to be bothered with any excess fluid." I remember at the time the whole thing seemed a little odd, but I really didn't think too much about it. I went to the bathroom and did as I was instructed. I then went back to bed and had just settled down but was by no means asleep, when I suddenly realized I was not alone. I saw the image of an alien standing beside my bed. He was bending over me from the waist at a slight angle. This alien figure appeared to be a projected image. It was completely stationary and had a snowy, "unreal" quality to it—like an old projector from the 1940s. It seemed as if you could put your hand right through it. I was so terrified. I cannot even begin to explain the raw fear I experienced. I have never felt such fear. To make matters worse, I was completely paralyzed. I couldn't move! I struggled to regain movement to no avail. I wanted to wake Rob. The only thing I had control over was my respiratory system, so I took full advantage of this and started panting as loudly as I could in order to wake him. I mentally screamed to the being, "NO! Go away!", over and over again. This hysterical panting and mental screaming scenario continued for about 30 seconds or so, and then the image disappeared and the experience was over. Robert, however, was awake the whole time. He had not yet fallen asleep when all this mess started. He had been looking out of the high vaulted windows and had never seen a thing. He heard me panting and had a feeling it might be alien connected, so he left me alone to see what would happen. Despite a thorough visual check, Robert never saw a thing; however, he did feel that something very unusual was happening. He felt the hair on the back of his neck stand on end. Immediately following the experience, I felt extremely shocked by the amount of fear potentially lurking in human beings. I was also very disappointed in myself for having been so rude to a being I didn't even know. I was very sad that I had handled the situation so poorly. An interesting side note to this story is that in January 1996, I read *Healing Shattered Reality* and it made reference to holographic imagery used in alien technology. This was the first literary encounter I had with the concept of holography. I immediately related it to the bedside alien experience. This is why I call it a holographic experience, although I feel it is important to note I had no such "education" on the concept of holography at the time of the incident.

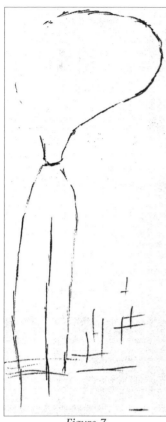

Figure 7

•it felt masculine

•it emitted a soft, white glow

•jumpsuit was skin-tight and same color as skin

•no visible wrinkles or other discernable skin qualities—skin seemed very smooth and had a luminous quality

•I was so surprised and utterly shocked by the extreme disproportion of the upper back part of the skull compared to that of a human head and to the relative size of the alien body

•I cannot remember the facial features. This is why I have sketched this area so vaguely.

•Because I was lying in bed, I couldn't see the being's lower body.

•It was short—because it was bent at the waist it is difficult to ascertain the height, but I would estimate it at 4-1/2 feet tall.

A few days after the holographic alien experience, we returned to our home in Texas and immediately left again to attend a week long conference in Nashville, Tennessee. My dear college friend, Kathy, came to our house to watch Alex for us while we were away. Kathy had a most unusual experience during her stay. Our home is out in the country, situated on a hill, overlooking a lake. In other words, from the windows of our living room, you have a view of the lake. On the evening of July 25th, Kathy put Alex to bed around 9:45 p.m. She then lay down on the couch, but couldn't fall asleep. For some unknown reason, Kathy was very anxious and unsettled. Finally, at 11:15 p.m., she decided to watch a video. It was over around 1:15 a.m., but she was still unable to calm herself, so she put in a second video. Between 1:30 a.m. and 2:00 a.m., while watching the movie, she saw something from the corner of her eye, green and glowing out over the lake. For a few seconds, it didn't register. Then she thought it was the VCR digital display reflecting off of the window, but then she realized this was not the case. She was very scared, but forced herself to go to the window, cupped her hands to her eyes and pressed her face to the glass. She saw a greenish glow in the shape of a diamond. It was bright and luminous; a "fuzzy glow" around it. It then started blinking randomly in a diamond pattern.It never really moved, the craft only hovered over the lake. Kathy thought to herself, "Think good thoughts", trying to keep her wits about her. She also felt that the aliens of the craft were able to pick up on her thoughts. She said to them, "I can't handle this. My body and mind are not able to handle this. I'm not the one you want. Theresa is the one you want". She stayed at the east window for 8-10 seconds longer and then decided she couldn't handle it any more. She walked away, sat down in a chair, and blankly stared at the TV screen for 20-30 seconds before she worked up the nerve to look out of the window again. When she did, the object was gone. She fell asleep within 30 minutes and slept fine for the rest of her stay.

I told my sister, Lisa, who at that time lived in Austin, Texas, about Kathy's experience. She suggested that I speak with someone educated in the field of astronomy. She gave me the name of an astronomer who was at that time employed by a highly respected university with a well known observatory. I gave him a call and recounted the incident. He told me that many so called "sightings" were very often only stars, planets, or other naturally occurring phenomena other than UFOs. He also told me that he was convinced that what Kathy saw was a UFO. He told me that the particular randomly blinking diamond shape had been reported numerous times. He also called Kathy and got her first-hand eyewitness account. On a closing note, he added that as an astronomer, he was convinced of the existence of extra-terrestrials and their subsequent craft.

There is one more story to be told about the rash of alien experiences during July 1993. I became pregnant with a child that I was unable to carry. Coincidentally, the conception occurred around July 5th, just at the time the "funny spot" on my back appeared. On July 30, 1993, the day we flew in from Nashville, Robert and I went to our family practitioner for the preliminary examination and ultrasound. At this time, the scar on my back was 3 weeks old and healing; however, the pattern of the wound was still visible. Robert showed our doctor the spot on my back and asked him what he thought it might be. Our doctor was puzzled and said he had never seen anything like it. He said it showed no characteristics of a bite, sting, or allergic reaction to a plant of any kind. Against my better judgement, Robert offered the idea of an alien induced wound as a possibility, as we both felt this might be the case due to the holographic experience as well as Kathy's sighting during the prior 2 weeks. Our doctor was absolutely horrified. He scolded us and told us that such things were evil and against God's plan, and that we should never discuss it again—with anyone! Our doctor is a very fine man and a fundamentalist Christian. Obviously, the idea of alien involvement is in direct conflict with his religious values. It was a very embarrassing and degrading experience.

Things were quiet for a while after this rash of experiences. It wasn't until November, 1993, that we were visited again. This time, however, it is Robert who has the story to tell. Robert and I were asleep in our master bedroom in Texas. Between 12:45 a.m. and 1:00 a.m., Alex woke up crying for no apparent reason, which was highly unusual, and she did not want to go back to sleep. Robert made several trips to her room to try to comfort her. Finally at 1:30 a.m. he decided to lie down with her in her room. He remained awake, waiting for her to fall back asleep so he could "sneak out". After about 20 minutes, Robert said, "It was like someone turned a switch on in my head". Suddenly there was an extremely loud and high frequency combination of sounds that sounded like a cross between a fax machine and a J. S. Bach symphony. The overall effect of the noise was more like a symphony. It was similar to Bach in that there were several separate, individual melodies within one complete synthesis. Each unique individual strain was separate within itself and discernable from the complete whole. It was like a fax machine in that it was high multi-frequencies —frequencies that tended to warble in and out of one another. It was neither analogue nor digital. It was a mix between instrumental (or analogue) and a fax machine (or digital). The noise seemed "placed" within Robert's brain because I didn't hear it, nor did Alex seem to. Robert said that it was so loud that under normal circumstances it would have broken his eardrum. It was also extremely clear, it seemed to bypass the normal imperfections and distortions of the anatomy of the human ear. The other reason Robert felt that it was "placed" in his brain is that he heard it in perfect stereo despite the fact that he was lying on his side with one ear muffled in a pillow. Although his eyes remained closed at all times, Robert has an unexplained sense of a being at the helm of controls 'monitoring the situation'. Robert also feels that he was given the idea telepathically that, "It would not be appreciated if you open your eyes or move".

The physical affect of this noise on Robert's body was most interesting. He said it made his body feel hypnotized/paralyzed. Robert didn't try to move so whether or not he was actually paralyzed is an unknown. But more importantly, Robert felt he did not have the need to move because the affect of the noise was incredibly relaxing, as if "the noise itself was massaging my spinal column". It seems analogous to "toning" techniques used by meditation practitioners in that Robert's body was completely relaxed. He felt as if he were in a mentally altered state, and he felt that he had unusual clarity of mind. He felt as if his mental state was heightened, although he described the sensation as a "mental dead calm". He was mentally hyper-alert and sensitive. This noise lasted about 30 seconds. When it was over, Robert remained motionless for about 5 seconds. He then got up and came into our master bedroom. He noted that the time was 3:00 a.m. He was very shocked by the missing time. Approximately one hour and 10 minutes were unaccounted for. During the experience, he never felt the bed nor Alex move. Rob, Alex and even the bed covers were in the exact same position they had been in before the "symphony". It is Robert's belief that something must have happened to me during this time, although I have no memory of anything unusual whatsoever.

The next unusual experience happened during 1994. I call it my "robbers dream". In the middle of the night, I was suddenly awakened by the presence of four "people" trying to get into our bedroom. We have glass doors on either side of our bed, one set leading out to the swimming pool, the other set to the driveway.

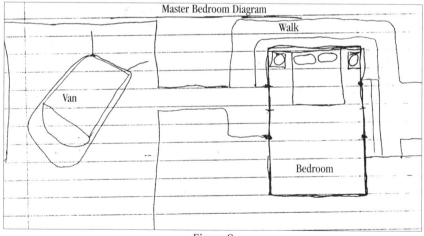

Figure 8

There were two figures at each set of glass doors. They stood motionless, looking in. These figures didn't "feel" right. Something seemed wrong; something seemed "off". For starters, they were all exactly the same height. The tops of their heads came to the top of the handles of the glass doors, which puts their height at 4 feet. They were all identical. The same build, the same height, and the same faces, although I can't remember what the faces looked like because they all had identical long, black, stringy, oily hair that partially obscured their faces. They were all dressed the same in black poncho-like coverings.

Mentally, I felt like I was wide awake, but completely paralyzed. I tried to scream for Robert, but I couldn't quite snap into reality. I remember wondering if I was actually getting words out of my mouth or not. I was absolutely terrified. I desperately wanted to know if Robert had locked the doors, because in my muddled, "drugged" state, I had the ridiculous notion that if the doors were locked, then everything would be okay. It felt like my body and my mind were not working right. Although I was wide awake, it all felt very "surrealistic". The next thing I remember is being loaded into a black van that was parked in the driveway. I don't remember how I got there. I was lying on my back, perhaps on something like a hospital gurney. As I was being situated inside the back of the van, I remember looking up around me at the interior of the van.It was cram-packed with instruments and electrical looking gadgets, none of which I recognized. I remember thinking that it reminded me of our corporate plane in that every square inch of space was completely utilized with equipment. The next thing I remember is walking barefoot in the caliche off the side of the asphalt beside the highway just before the entrance to our driveway. I remember picking and choosing my path carefully because of small water puddles. It was very dark outside, but somehow there was vague light for me to see by. That is the end of my dream. There are a couple of side notes to be mentioned. The next day, I told Robert about my "weird" dream, not really thinking too much about it. Robert is the one who immediately made the possible alien connection, not me. Robert also told me that during the night of my dream it had been misting heavily. He said that I was not even aware that it had misted because it was sunny and the moisture had evaporated by the time I got up, got Alex and myself dressed and fed. Very interesting.

The next unusual event occurred in mid-December, 1995, although before I begin, a quick briefing is in order. In November of 1995, one month prior to the next unusual experience, we had a prowler on our property. A brush pile out back had been deliberately burned. I called the police, an officer was dispatched, and a report was made. During this time, Robert had been out of town 90% of the time.

In our business, we employ several hundred people so we must always take into account the possibility of disgruntled employees. I was understandably aware of the possibility of further incidents and was extra alert and aware due to the fact that Robert was out of town and I alone had the responsibility for the safety and well being of myself and Alex.

The actual "other worldly" incident occurred one month later. It was around midnight and I had just fallen asleep when I was suddenly awakened by a loud thump behind my headboard on the outside wall of the house. I immediately sat upright in bed, wide awake, alert, and terrified that whoever had burned the brush was back on the property and I felt Alex and I were in danger. I knew by the loud noise and by the force of the thump on the wall that it couldn't possibly have been an animal. I was racing options though my mind and decided that I should call 911 immediately. All of this happened in a matter of 5 seconds, and then suddenly, before I could physically respond to any decision I had made, I suddenly felt drugged. I remained conscious for only about 5 seconds, but I was in an altered state of consciousness. In this "drugged", altered state, I was very intimate with the feeling I was having. It felt very familiar and I thought to myself as I slumped to my pillow, "Damn it! They've done it to me again!". I also felt as if my upper thighs had changed their molecular structure. They felt as if they were being pushed down into the mattress, like they were becoming a part of the mattress. I believe the result was that my upper body was subsequently elevated. This is the last thing I remember.

The following month, on January 3, 1996, Alex had a UFO sighting, although at the time she had no name for it. She was four years and six weeks old when it happened. It was a clear, sunny afternoon around 2:00 p.m. I drove just into the entrance of our driveway, put the emergency brake on, and proceeded to go to the mail box to check the mail. As I got out of the car, Alex stopped me. She was sitting up front in the passenger's seat and had pivoted herself around to face the driver's door and side window so that her eyes might follow me to the mail box. She was facing due west. Her vantage point was rather restricted. She only had the view out of the driver's side window. As I closed the car door, she pointed out of the window and said, "Look, Mommy! What is that?" I saw absolutely nothing. I noticed other cars driving by and noted that they obviously didn't see anything either. Alex kept saying, "It's right there, Mommy. Don't you see it?" She became frustrated with me because I didn't see it also. She described it

81

as round and silver with "sticking out things". These sticking out things she later compared to the brim of a hat. She also said it had three red/orange lights. She said it zigged and zagged erratically about. She watched it for about 3 minutes. I finally drove up the driveway and went inside. I suppose it eventually went away! She said it was not an airplane (and she should know since she is very familiar with them) or a helicopter. Alex had never been exposed to any of our unusual experiences. We have been very careful to keep her out of ear shot of our conversations nor had she been exposed to any UFO/alien literature. She had no idea what she was seeing. Interestingly, a few months later we happened to catch Walt Andrus, International Director for MUFON in Seguin, Texas, on a television program. He was explaining a little bit about MUFON (Mutual UFO Network), and in the background had a model of the typical "flying saucer". Alex lit up like a candle. She jumped up and down with excitement and said, "Did you hear, Mommy? It's called a UFO! That's the same thing I saw!." She was so pleased to have a name for the craft she saw, and at that point, any self doubts were, for the moment, washed away. Now my daughter was involved and I knew I had to find help to deal with our experiences. I called a well known UFO researcher and told him of our experiences. He told me there was no doubt in his mind that I was an abductee and he gave me the name of a man who worked with experiencers. This began a search which eventually led to Constance Clear with the hope of memory recovery via hypnotherapy. As it turns out, I am not a good hypnotic subject. I think I have so many doubts about the ideologies of hypnotherapy that subconsciously I don't allow myself to participate. It seems to work for some people, but not for me. Fortunately, however, Constance has been very helpful for me in other ways—perhaps more important ways. Her clear thinking, logical analysis, and most importantly, open-mindedness has been a tremendous source of encouragement and a catalyst for continued intuitive and soulful inquiry.

How have these experiences impacted my life? Well, it has made for a very interesting marriage, and I actually feel it has enriched our relationship. The experiences have been a catalyst for searching for some very important answers about life, love, religion, and any other fascinating and meaningful concept under the sun. These experiences have shown us aspects of one another we might never have otherwise discovered. I love my husband so very much, and I am so grateful to have him by my side encouraging and supporting me every step of the way. With the exception of a few dear friends and family members, we discuss these experiences with no one. I am very grateful for those few friends with whom I have decided to share our stories. They have helped me grow and stretch my intellect and spirituality with their keen insights, interpretations, suggestions, and unconditional love. My parents support me as well, although they are a little reserved about the whole thing. My sisters find it extremely interesting and are always passing on bits of information they have gleaned from TV or literature with great enthusiasm. How much luckier could I possibly be?

How have these experiences impacted my world view? Perhaps because I don't have conscious recollection, I have the luxury of calling it interesting. I cling to the hope that prophetic and spiritual knowledge lie trapped in my subconscious, although by no means do I feel this knowledge would replace God or the loving teachings of Christ. I feel quite certain that God's plan is ever-expansive and utterly impossible to contain or pinpoint. Perhaps the other worldly experiences are yet another aspect of God we are only now on the brink of discovering. We must never forget that we have a tool at our disposal to help us contemplate this phenomena: history. It is important to remember that just because something has yet to be scientifically proven does not negate its reality. Medieval alchemists would have found it utterly impossible to fathom a world of micro-organisms invisible to the naked eye, although today it is accepted without question as general knowledge. I hope that we are not so arrogant to think that we have completed our educational,technological, intellectual, and spiritual development. Perhaps the most important thing I have learned from these experiences is to hold other human beings in awe. What fabulous, interesting, and potentially limitless beings we really are if we only allow ourselves to be. Once we rid ourselves of the confining shield of "not possible", we open ourselves to new wonders and glories of God we had never even imagined. Whenever I see the girl next door, I smile and marvel at the human being as an infinite expression of the "all that is". Isn't that what God said when he created us?

Note from Constance:

It has been nine months since Theresa wrote her story. Five months ago she made another attempt to be hypnotized. I witnessed the session, and though the hypnotherapist used some very elegant techniques, Theresa's unconscious mind held its ground. The more he suggested she relax, the more diligent she became in defense of some invisible perimeter. It was agonizing to watch her struggle. It was as though her conscious mind had drawn a line in the sand beyond which she could not go.

All along, I had a theory as to why Theresa's unconscious mind had taken this stance. For several years I have worked with another woman whom I believe to be an experiencer, though we don't often discuss it. I have invited her to the Friday Night Group, but so far she has not come. Both women have responded in the same psychological fashion. What they have in common is that each is the mother of a young daughter, and both girls are reporting UFO related experiences.

Any parent reading this knows that there is nothing more painful than knowing your child is suffering and you are helpless to stop it. This may not be the time in these women's lives to tamper with their defenses. As my husband says, "When you run up against Mother Nature, you have only two choices. you get out of the way or you get trampled."

Theresa wrote an update to her story when the group gathered on July 8, 1997. Based on her daughter, Alex's, recent experiences I don't believe my theory is off-base. Watching Theresa and Robert deal with their own experiences has been one thing, but watching them deal with Alex's unfolding drama is quite another. But for all the trauma this family has endured, I must say that they are all three delightful to be around. I got to interview Alex about her UFO sighting in March of 1996. She is an impressive, articulate child with an unusual degree of self composure. It is as though she is completely comfortable with herself. She recently swam the length of the lake near their home without stopping as her daddy swam along beside her. She covered a distance of one-half mile.

Theresa's Update: Written July 1997

A few months have gone by since I wrote the story that you have just read. One Wednesday afternoon in May 1997, a good girlfriend and I took our daughters swimming. During the course of the swim, my friend gasped and blurted out, "Oh my gosh! What happened to Alex's leg?" I looked at her leg and for the first time noticed a large, deep, rectangular wound behind her knee. It was a clear, yellow serum scab—obviously it had never bled. We asked Alex what had happened, and she said it was a burn. When we asked her how she got the burn, she had no recall and was unable to answer the question. She said she had first noticed it Saturday, four days earlier. Alex can usually tell you about every scrape on her body and how she got it, yet this large gaping wound remained an enigma. It should have bled profusely and would have required stitches had it been caught immediately. It healed in a very peculiar manner: it changed from a rectangle to a circle.

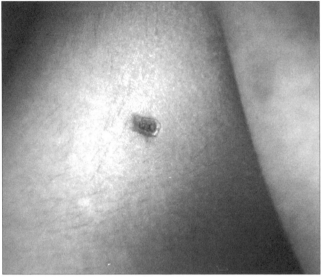

Figure 9

In mid July, we believe that Alex was visited again. When she woke up in the morning and climbed in bed with me for our ritualistic morning cuddle, her form-fitting night gown was not on properly. It was over her head properly, but an arm hole had been missed—it wasn't that she had wiggled out of it in the night—the neck line and entire right sleeve was under her arm. It was uncomfortable to her and was cutting into her neck. She was very confused about it and had no idea how it had happened. I asked her to take the gown off and duplicate it. She couldn't. I had to help her, and even for me it was a tight squeeze and a struggle. I think that these two aforementioned incidents show that Alex is definitely involved, and I believe that this is the beginning of a relationship that will last throughout her lifetime. I worry for her—I only pray that it will not be traumatic for her, as it seems to be for others. I have offered no suggestions to her as to what I think this might be. This is not my place, nor is it my right. She must come to her own realization in her own time. When and if this realization occurs—I will give her the journal that I have been keeping on her, myself, and our family. Hopefully her generation will be one of love and understanding and perhaps more answers will unfold during this time.

About a month later Alex spontaneously drew this picture for me. When she handed it to me she said, "Mommy, I drew an alien for you." What do you think...?

Figure 10

Note from Constance:

I had hoped that Robert would write something for the book so that you could get a feel for him. A man of amazing talent, he literally designs and builds complete architectural projects without plans. I've seen the results and they are exquisite. Having him participate in the Friday Night Group with his curiosity and quick wit has been a definite asset. Robert is able to enliven even the most serious discussions.

In November of 1997, I had the opportunity to interview Robert on the subject of his feelings about his family's involvement in all of this.

Robert started out the interview saying that he began to figure out something was going on about two years into his marriage to Theresa. He said when he saw the movie *Fire In The Sky*, he felt that the story was probably true and things began to fall into place. He had noticed strange things happening in the house and Theresa says he was the one who got her to open her eyes and begin questioning what was going on.

I asked Robert how he felt about his wife and his daughter being taken and he said it didn't bother him. "They haven't hurt anybody," he continued, explaining that he liked being "part of the experiment, part of something beyond our technology." He said it has made him "question reality in the way it's presented." He feels like he's at the cutting edge of evolution, of human consciousness. He added, "It's better than going out buying new cars to impress our neighbors."

It is Robert's belief that humans are a young species and that our strength lies in our individuality. He says that variation is crucial to our survival. I don't know whether or not he's right about that, but I do know Robert has been crucial to Theresa's survival.

Chapter Five

A Haunted Life

Prologue to Andrew's Story

Andrew, age sixty, was the fifth of the seven to find his way into my office. Andrew knew of me through my husband. I knew that Andrew was a retired drafting teacher who loved woodworking. What I did not know was that he had experienced a lifetime of anxiety, depression, and panic attacks.

Andrew called in the spring of 1996 wanting to explore a memory that had "nagged" and "worried" him for fifty-four years. It had seemed so real that he had never been satisfied with his mother's explanation that it was a dream. He remembered something that happened when he was staying at his grandfather's house when he was six. He had gotten up in the night to go to the bathroom and when he looked through the kitchen, he saw twelve ghosts arranged in stair step order outside the windows. He also remembered a little girl with blond hair who was crying.

Andrew had received therapy from another practitioner, and had worked out many personal issues, but he continued to have periodic panic attacks followed by days of deep depression. His physician had prescribed medication for anxiety, which he took as needed, but his nightly dread of going to bed had not abated.

Andrew knew of my work as a hypnotherapist, and asked if hypnosis could be used to explore his memory. It took Andrew two sessions to relive what turned out to be a terrifying alien abduction experience, the first of many. Andrew proved to be an exceptional hypnotic subject. He was able to go into trance easily and he proceeded to relive in real time, everything he has seen, thought, felt, and been told. It was compelling and sometimes agonizing to witness.

During those first two sessions, it did not seem as though I was listening to a sixty-year-old man recalling an experience from childhood. Instead, it was an though he was a terrified and stubborn six-year-old boy who was mentally fighting his captors with every fiber of his being. Of course he proved no match for them and after reliving a terribly painful procedure on what he referred to as his "dinky worm," he said, with tears flowing from his left eye, "My mother is gonna whip me for letting them do this to me".

When I brought Andrew out of trance, I realized that for over an hour, he had been digging his fingernails into the back of his other hand. In subsequent sessions I learned to incorporate a suggestion that Andrew would not relive physical sensations of pain, but would view his experience as though watching it on a screen. This eliminated his writhing in the chair, but not his emotional distress.

At the conclusion of our third session, I suggested that Andrew write about his experiences hoping, it would help him work through his feelings. Little did I know that he would also draw everything he had seen. I later found out that Andrew had worked part-time, for several years, as an engineering draftsman, sketching airplane parts that were being modified. He frequently had to crawl into tiny spaces inside an airplane parked in a hanger, where temperatures sometimes exceeded 100 degrees. He trained himself to study the part and go inside the air conditioned building to finish drawing it.

At one point in his therapy, Andrew devised a test to check his ability to accurately draw something no longer in front of him. He opened a book and looked at a picture of an airplane for ten seconds. Ten hours later he drew it from memory. Andrew seemed reassured by the results. As you can see, the two pictures are almost identical.

Figure 11   *Figure 12*

Most of the following accounts were written by Andrew following his hypnotic sessions. Three of the sessions were tape recorded and the actual transcripts are included. The remaining sessions are documented by the notes I took during the respective sessions. They are presented in the order that they emerged into consciousness through his sessions with me.

The following is Andrew's written account of his first abduction experience as recalled through two hypnotic regressions. Though he described his encounter in the present tense while in trance, he switches between past and present tense when reporting it.

Ghosts at the Window

Date of Incident: 1942 Date of Sessions: April 9, 1996 and April 10, 1996

During the year of 1942, I was living in San Antonio at my grandparent's home with my mother. One night I had to go to the bathroom which was down the hall and past the kitchen. As I was returning to the bedroom, I happened to look into the kitchen. The kitchen was a large room with six single-hung windows at the back. As I looked at the windows, I saw what I thought were twelve ghosts.

They were standing according to their height from tallest to the shortest. All of the ghosts looked alike. They were very skinny with large heads and large black, slanted, almond-shaped eyes. There was a rim of skin around their eyes and their eyes didn't blink. Just a cold stare. They were grayish-white in color.

Figure 13

As I stood there I realized I could not move and could not say anything. I saw the middle ghost move through the closed window and he came toward me. At this point, I became scared and began to cry. I noticed that he had no ears, his head was egg shaped. He had only two small holes for his nose and his mouth was very small. His eyes seemed to be multi-eyed, like an insect. He reached out and grabbed my hand. I saw that he had three long fingers. All were very skinny, bony and long. The three fingers were the same length. There was a thumb. It was very small and it looked like a nub (Figure 14). His hand was cool to the touch. Both of us passed through the closed window without breaking it. We seemed to float in the night sky. As we floated up, I saw a large object which I could vaguely make out. The next thing that I knew was that I was in a huge room. It looked to be two stories high. The room was very bright and I could not tell where the light was coming from. The wall and ceiling seemed to glow. The room looked like a fourth of a circle (Figure 16).

The room smelled bad...musky. As I looked around, I saw about fifteen children at the door between what I thought was an information panel and some compartments (Figure 15).

There were children of both sexes and all races, including black, brown and white. They looked scared and were crying. All of the children were nude. Most of them seemed to be in shock. There was no movement. Some held their heads down. A little girl with blonde hair was lying on a metal table and she was also nude and crying (at this point, all communication is carried out telepathically).

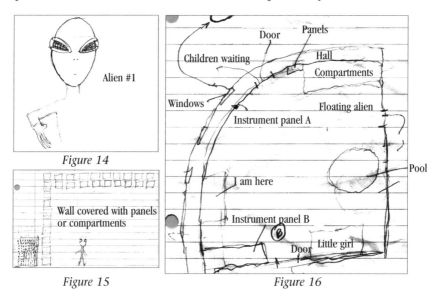

Figure 14

Figure 15

Figure 16

Alien #1

Wall covered with panels or compartments

Door — Panels

Children waiting

Hall

Compartments

Windows

Floating alien

Instrument panel A

I am here

Pool

Instrument panel B

Door — Little girl

The alien that brought me into this ship took off my clothes and cut off a piece of my pajamas and removed a button. Through my tears, I thought, "Boy are you in trouble now with my mother. She is going to be very mad at you". He told me that he didn't care.

Now two more aliens came into the room. One looked like the others that I described earlier. The other one was different. He had more of a human skull. His eyes were large, elliptical shape and straight. Both eyes seemed to wrap around his head and they had a rim around them. He had a small nose and a small mouth. There were wrinkles between the eyes and none of the aliens had hair. His color was gray (Figure 17). This was the mean one. He was the one that ran all the tests on me and the little blonde girl. He seemed to be the leader.

I told one of the other aliens to leave me and the little blonde girl alone. He told me to stop thinking and I told him I didn't have to. He told me if I didn't stop thinking he would turn me over to the alien that they had floating in front of the cabinets (Figure 18). He told me that this alien is very, very bad and mean. I didn't think they would turn me over to him because they seemed afraid of him.

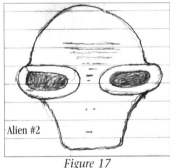

Figure 17

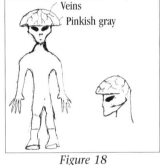

Figure 18

They made me lie down on this table. As I look back on this table, I believe the objects under the tables were different types of sensors and information was fed to the information panel (See "A" on Figure 16).

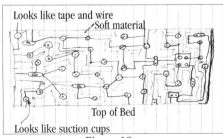

Figure 19

At this point, I was still thinking and all of a sudden I was placed in darkness and I didn't know if I had been transported to another room for isolation or what happened. I felt that a cover over the table had been dropped over me. After what seemed forever, I was brought back to the light (Figure 20).

Then the alien #2 leaves and takes out some instruments from a cabinet (See "B" on Figure 16). The first instrument he held in his hand had a wire that ran from the part he held and it had a small plug on the end. The plug was placed inside my ear. It hurt badly. I am really crying now. After awhile, it was removed and a sample of ear wax was removed.

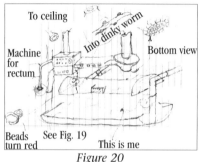

Figure 20

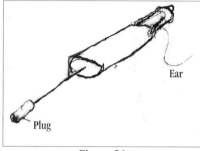

Figure 21

He also cut a piece of my hair off and, with a sharp instrument, he scraped off some skin. He removed tear samples, and with another instrument, he looked into my eye ball. At this point, I am afraid of going blind. Another instrument was run into my nose. It was hand-held and had a place he could look into. One end of the instrument was plugged into the machine over the table. The other end was fed into my nose. This really hurt my nose. Tissue and blood samples were taken from my nose, and my nose began to bleed.

He took the ear instrument and exchanged the plug at the end and replaced it with an object that had three balls on it about the size of a dime. One ball was white, the next one was black and the third one was silver. At the end of the silver one, there was an object that looked like a bear claw. This end was fed into my mouth and down my throat. It hurt my stomach. It made me gag as the wire moved down my throat. Again, samples were taken.

Figure 22

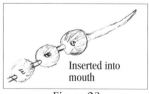

Figure 23

94

During this time, as I looked up from the table I could see an object that was round and had many different colors in the center and around the outside of the circle many colors moved around it. Each color that moved around the outside had a beam shining down on my head. I don't know what they were doing, but I got a headache. Next they moved me on my stomach and ran an object into my rear end. Samples were taken again, I saw the leader hand them to one of the other aliens. All of the samples were handed to him and he placed them in a rack. The one who was taking the samples also took a piece of my fingernail and removed some material from under the nail.

I am placed on my back again and this time they take an object from the machine and clamp something around my dinky-worm (penis). The clamp is placed behind the head. After this was done, something was run into it. I tell them, "Stop. This is hurting", and I feel tears, again run down my face. I can see what looked like beads and they all turn red. I can tell the leader does not like this.

At this point, they left me and began to work on the little girl. I told her to fight them but she does not move or say anything to me. She seems to be in a very deep sleep. I knew this girl. She was Cyan. She lived in the city I had just left where we were in school together. She was my first girlfriend. But how did she get in San Antonio? Now I am very mad. How could they do this to her? I want to stop them but I can't move, no matter how hard I try.

After her testing, they do something really strange. The leader comes back to me and I feel myself floating, but my body is still on the table and I can see my body. I am being floated over to Cyan. The next thing that comes to my mind is the alien asking me what I like. I said, "Airplanes", and he didn't believe it. At this point, he asked the question again and I said, "Dolls". He said, "That's better". The machine with the colors now really went crazy and I got a bad headache. After awhile, I am back in my body. One of the aliens is putting on my clothes. He then took me over to the dark hole shown on the floor plan, and the next thing I know, I am back in my grandparents' house.

The next morning I told my mother, and she told me that I had a nightmare. I said I can prove it. They took a button and a piece of my nightwear. But, when I looked down, nothing was missing.

Locked in the Shop

Date of Incident: May 17, 1996 Date of Session: May 21, 1996

Note from Constance:

Following our first two sessions, I was in Australia for a month as an Ambassador of Goodwill for Rotary International. I made sure Andrew had the name of the therapist covering for me during my absence. The night of my return, Andrew was visited again.

When he called me to make an appointment, he told me he was afraid he was losing his mind. He had gone to bed as usual the night before, only to wake up locked in his wood shop at 3:00 in the morning. When he got back inside his house, he discovered that his underwear was on inside out and backwards. The following is Andrew's account written after his hypnotic regression.

That night I felt real tired so I went to sleep early. Later that night, I felt a presence in my room. It was the alien I saw many years ago. He was standing between my dresser and the door. I felt like I wanted to get out of the room, but he was standing in my way. I found out that I could not move. He told me that it had been a long time and it was time again for more tests. I told him that I didn't want to go, and he told me that I didn't have a choice. I told him it's my body and I did have a choice. He told me that was really not so. He reached out and touched me, and the next thing that I knew was that we were going through the aluminum sliding window. Again, the window did not break. I noticed my dogs in the back yard, and they acted like they didn't see me. In fact, they just stood there. I thought, "Some watch dogs, they didn't even bark". The next thing I saw was a large ship just above the Mesquite trees. It was blacked out and you had to be up close to see it.

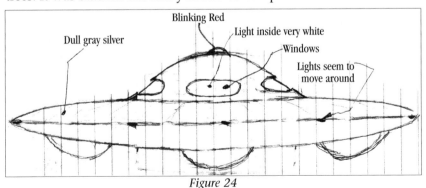

Figure 24

At this point, we went under the ship and into a dark entrance. Again, I found myself in that bright clean room. The alien removed my underwear and I was placed on a table. Again there was a musky smell.

Alien #2 entered the room. He has two instruments with him. The first was like the instrument he used on my ears in the previous abduction. Again, he ran the instrument into my ear. It hurt my ear terribly. I thought I might lose my hearing. I became very frightened as I do not like anything in my ears. My doctor will tell you that. Through out my life I have been treated for ear infections.

The second instrument was new. It had a cover like a condom. Built into the condom was a metal ring. One side of the ring was open with prongs like an o-ring. There were three wires that came from it. Those wires joined and went to a cylinder that was approximately 6" long. From there it went to a small container. The container had a tube with a sharp needle.

The condom part of the instrument fit over my penis and the prongs of the ring fit just behind the head. The prongs dug into the foreskin of my penis and caused a great pain.

The instrument was used like a milking machine, which caused me to have a climax. The semen was collected into the small cylinder. At this point, alien #2 became very upset because he figured out that I'd had a vasectomy. He took the needle and stuck it into my scrotum. I felt the needle enter one of my testicles. Again, the device drew semen from me. It felt like I had been hit with a hard ball, and I wanted to double up, but I couldn't move. This procedure almost drove me out of my mind with pain. At this point I must have blacked out, because I don't remember them removing the instrument.

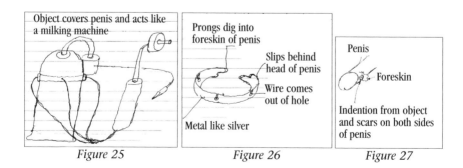

Object covers penis and acts like a milking machine

Prongs dig into foreskin of penis

Slips behind head of penis

Wire comes out of hole

Metal like silver

Penis

Foreskin

Indention from object and scars on both sides of penis

Figure 25   *Figure 26*   *Figure 27*

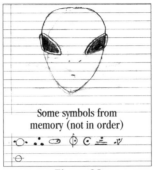

Some symbols from
memory (not in order)

Figure 28

After the test, I was removed from the table and alien #1 led me to what seemed to be a wall. He told me that I shouldn't remember what goes on behind that wall. It would act like a blocking device to my mind. On the wall there were three rows of hieroglyphics.

After much fighting with my mind, the wall was removed. Again I was placed on a table. Beside me was another table and I saw a blonde woman who I recognized as Cyan, but she is much older. Again, they removed me from my body and my feelings and thoughts are transferred to Cyan's body. At this point, alien #2 moved away from me and went to the compartments. He pulled one open and removed a baby from it. The baby did not appear to be earthly. It was skinny and sickly. Alien #2 seemed to place the baby into Cyan's body. At this point, I felt like Cyan's body was being ripped apart. The pain was terrible, almost unbearable. I think the aliens were testing my feeling under childbirth. The aliens had lines leading from my brain to hers and from hers to mine. There was also a line leading to a wall plug. After what seemed forever, our feelings and minds were switched back.

Alien #1 rotated the table to a vertical position. All of the lights were turned off except for a screen. They began to show me images of the Earth exploding. Rocks and other debris were shown in 3-D holograms. My body and mind were pushed to the limits with fear. After a while, the lights were turned on again and the switch of feelings and mind was performed and the same test was run again. Again, fear occurs, but much more intense. After this, the switch back was made, alien #1 removed me from the table and put on my underwear. At this point, we went through a dark hole in the ship.

The next thing I remember was waking up lying on the floor in my hot wood shop. The big floor fan was running and the lights were on. I had sawdust all over me. I got up and found that the door was locked. However, the dead bolt thumb lock was the only one locked. That's odd, I remember locking both locks earlier. As I opened the door, I was still puzzled. Where are my dogs, they must be hiding somewhere for I do not see them. I walk to the house and find it locked.

I remembered that I had a key hidden outside in the covered patio. I opened the door and heard the grandfather clock strike 3:00 a.m. Needless to say, I found myself in a world of confusion. I went to take a shower and found that my underwear was on inside out and backwards.

Camp Luis Farr

Date of Incident: 1949 Date of Session: June 1996

Note from Constance:

Andrew began this session talking about the experiences he had as a youth living on Goodfellow Air Force Base. In the summer of 1949 he remembered stepping out on the porch of his base housing at 1:00 pm and seeing three UFO's streak across the sky in a southwest direction, flying in a V formation. They were white and they left no vapor trails. This incident occurred the same year that a civilian search and rescue pilot, Kenneth Arnold, flying near Mt. Rainier, reported seeing nine boomerang shaped UFO's flying in formation and traveling at an estimated speed of 1700 miles per hour.

Andrew spent a great deal of time studying aircraft as a child and he knew that we didn't have anything that could fly that fast. While living on Goodfellow AFB, Andrew used to sneak out and photograph the aircraft that landed at the base, and on more than one occasion, the MP's stopped him and took the film from his camera. But Andrew, as you may already realize, is not easily deterred, and his encounters with the MP's did not put a stop to his picture-taking activities.

Andrew had a feeling that something might have happened to him during the time he lived on base, although there was no obvious clue to trace. What follows is Andrew's written account of what he recalled during this hypnotic regression. He wrote this account several months later, utilizing notes I had taken during the session, so that the episode could be included in this book. You will notice that he tells this story in the present tense which is consistent with the way he reported his experience while under hypnosis.

It is the summer of 1949, and our Boy Scout unit has planned a survival weekend camp out at Camp Luis Farr. The trip to the camp was normal for a group of young scouts.

Upon arriving, we set up our camp for the night. A campfire was set up in the middle of the camp. Two scouts were assigned to each tent (one beginning scout, Tenderfoot, and one advanced scout, Star, or above). Our first scare that night was a mountain lion. We heard it scream in the distance. The scream of the mountain lion sounded like a woman screaming. The second was some animal running through the leaves in our camp. The third was the ultimate in the state of terror. Almost within the blink of an eye, this thing (that I now know was a gray) comes through the canvas without even cutting it. As soon as I see him, I try to scramble out of the tent, but I can't move. Am I scared stiff? I hear the other boy in the tent yell, "Hit it, Hit it". I feel that his yell will awaken the others in our camp, but no one comes to our assistance. This thing stands about four feet high with a big head and small body. It is gray in color with black, almond-shaped eyes. Mentally, it tells me I must go with him.

The next thing that happens is that we (the gray and I) are inside of a large bluish tunnel. I can see out. They are not taking the other scout. I see him frozen with his mouth open. I am thinking, "Why are they not taking him?" We are now moving upward through the top of the tent and out into the night. Momentarily, I see all of the tents below and there is no one outside of them. In a flash (just like a camera flash), I find myself in a room. It is ivory white in here. There are no shadows and the room glows like phosphorus. It stinks in here. It's a very bad musky smell.

As I look around, I see three of these ugly shapes in the room. One of these I have seen before when I was much smaller. They are telling me that they must remove my clothes. After my clothes are removed, they place me on a table. The table is glowing white, and my form is marked out on the table. One of these ugly forms is very close to me. His eye seems only a fraction of an inch from mine. He seems to be probing my mind with his eye. I become extremely exhausted. It isn't painful, but very tiring and draining. He is absorbing every thought and all the knowledge that I have. I feel like I am in a vegetative state. Mentally he tells me I must do this for them and that it is my fault they must do this. I don't understand that statement and he does not supply an answer even though I ask him several times. His eye is still peering into mine. I feel we are one. It feels like his eye is being stamped into my brain. I am scared to death. His eye is like a bottomless pit. If there is pain, his eye seems to have a soothing effect and it calms me down. Again he stresses we have to have this information. I don't understand. I want to ask questions but I can't. I tell him I'm only a kid. There are others that know much more than I do. Now his eye begins to move away from mine and I begin to feel more like myself. I can now ask questions. I ask him why this was done? He tells me they need it for their own benefit.

He is now putting something on my arm. It looks like a ring around my elbow. He touches the ring and seems to gather information when he touches it. The ring looks like plastic. I ask him what he is doing, but I receive no answer. I ask about his leader and he tells me "It's just us."

Something is being stuck in my other arm (my right arm). It looks like a needle with a bulb on the end of it. The bulb is clear and it hurts my arm. They need to draw fluid from my body. They need blood.

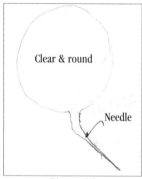

Clear & round

Needle

Figure 29

He is asking me to sit up. This is stupid, I can't move. They place me in a sitting position. He touches the back of my head with his finger, then runs it across the bottom of my foot. He is concerned that I'm not ticklish. Now they are talking together. The same one comes back and tries the other foot. I tell him, "Maybe I'm not ticklish because I can't feel anything." I can't move.

He looks at my big toe. (I have had a history of real bad ingrown toenails). He questions me about my ingrown toenail and he thinks I'm lying to him. He penetrates my mind to see if I'm telling him the truth. He withdraws his eye again and they talk to each other in a high pitched hum. Another needle is placed in my arm. He tells me they need a bone and muscle sample.

They stand me up on my feet and dress me. They tell me it is time to leave. I ask him how many times they are going to take me, and they tell me that they don't know what will be required by them later on.

I'm placed in a dark hole and find myself back in the tent. I ask my friend if he saw anything and he tells me I'm just dreaming. He remembers the rustling leaves outside of the tent. Then he says, "If anybody came through the tent, they would have to use the door." He says I was only having a nightmare.

Missing Miles

Date of Incident: June 1996 Date of Session: June 27, 1996
Note from Constance:

Andrew spent this session exploring something that happened as he and his wife were driving through west Texas on their way to a family funeral. They suddenly realized that they had missed driving through the town of Wellington. When they arrived at their destination, Andrew noticed they were 45 minutes late and the trip odometer, that he faithfully sets, was 52.6 miles short of the distance from here to his in-laws house.

Needless to say, Andrew was beside himself as he had now realized that these beings could come get him anytime...anywhere. His wife decided she didn't want to know what had happened to them as she already felt overwhelmed by other problems. But as usual, Andrew had to know.

 Eight months later, while compiling information for this book, neither Andrew nor I could find any notes from this session. I did have the drawing (Figure 30) that Andrew had given me soon after the session. To refresh his memory before writing a narrative, Andrew asked if he could be hypnotized a second time to explore the same experience. That session was held on February 20, 1997.

As I was to learn, repeat hypnosis often yields new material. It's as though the unconscious mind allows certain bits or portions of the experience to surface as we are ready to receive them. The events Andrew recalled on February 20, 1997 began and ended exactly as I remembered him describing them during our June 27th session, only this time, a heretofore unknown middle part of the experience emerged. Because of its highly emotional content, I could understand why Andrew had not remembered this part months earlier. Actually I'm grateful that he didn't, as I believe it would have overwhelmed him at the time.

Included here is the portion of Andrew's narrative describing what he remembered during the session held on June 27, 1996. The remaining, and more disturbing part of the encounter, is included in the section titled Missing Miles: Second Regression.

The first three-fourths of our trip to Wheeler was uneventful. That would be from San Antonio to Childress, Texas. In our wildest dreams, my wife and I would never have envisioned that we would go through the fear and horror of an alien abduction, in the last leg of our trip. Highway 83 is not a well-traveled highway (from Childress to Wheeler). The last thing I remember is leaving the Childress city limits and setting the speed control in my Lincoln at 70 MPH.

From this point onward, everything was brought out through hypnosis. The next thing I see is a green and white street sign stating 83 North. I am being told to turn off the highway. I notice that there is nothing out here, only brush and hedge rows of elm. My car stops and I feel like I am being squeezed and pulled from my car. At this point, I wonder where my wife is. I can see my car parked on a very narrow shoulder. The next thing I remember is that I find myself in an ultra bright lighted room. At this point, I see three aliens that are in the room. One I know very well, as he has come for me in other abductions. He is working on some equipment. He seems very disturbed as the equipment isn't working like he wants it to. I find that I can't move and I am floating in mid air. The other aliens are removing my clothes. I don't like this.

They are running some more tests on my sex organs. I can't see what they are doing and I don't understand why they are so interested in my penis.

I still see them working on the equipment that I saw when I first came into the room. They seem to be working on a time-altering machine to correct the missing time in an abduction.

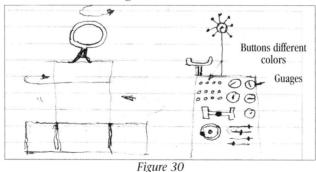

Figure 30

103

I am being told that it's time to return to my car (which they call a capsule) since we cannot help. When I get in the car, my wife is sleeping. With some difficulty, I am able to start the car, get back onto Highway 83, and continue to our destination.

In a short time, I see the skyline of a town. I tell my wife that we are approaching Wellington, Texas in case she wants to stop. She looks at the skyline and says that it's Shamrock. I say no because we haven't traveled through Wellington. We are still traveling at 70 m.p.h. In a few miles, I see Shamrock's city limits. We are confused at this point because neither of us have any memory of passing through Wellington. How could we go 70 m.p.h. through a town? Within 30 minutes, we arrive at my mother-in-law's home. My estimated time of arrival was 6:15. It is now 7:00. Later, I checked my odometer and it states 449.4 miles, which is 52.6 miles short of what it should be.

Note from Constance:

As Andrew's therapy progressed and he realized the extent to which these beings had intervened in his life against his will, he became increasingly distraught. In hope of easing his distress, I asked Andrew to write an essay for me describing what it was like for him to live with his experiences. This is what he wrote:

Andrew's First Essay: What Do I Do?

I have a secret that I can tell only to a select few. A secret that was forced upon me without my consent. A terrible secret that I must live and relive the rest of my life. There are a select few that I have told, but how can they believe me when I have trouble believing it myself?

As I live with this secret, I have periods of doubts about my mental health. Am I insane or going insane? I know others would think I am insane. A secret that tends to destroy my self-worth and makes me feel substandard to others. My guard must always be up and even at that, I feel that others may detect what I know. I must be extremely careful in what I say or do. Someone in the select few that I told said, "I was so fortunate". Believe me, such is not the case. It is a secret that no one should endure. If my secret does come out, my name cannot be used for fear of being ridiculed.

Insomnia, anxiety attacks, detachment, recurrent dreams and depression are all my unwelcome friends. Dealing with this secret is so painful and the suffering is so great that my mind and body feel they will explode and tears of pain and fear will pour down my face. My mind continues to fight in order not to give up the secret by setting up blocks. Only those who have gone through the rape of an alien abduction can understand the problems of which I speak. We know that we do not have a life of our own and that we can be abducted at any time and any place again and again only to relive more pain and more suffering at the hands of the aliens. There is no protection for us.

Note from Constance:

Witnessing Andrew's distress finally motivated me to start a support group for my pioneer clients...our human ambassadors, as I've come to think of them. I did this in spite of the fact that five days after my return from Australia, I learned that my mother was dying of ovarian cancer, and I was flying out of state every other week to be with her.

The first group meeting was held on July 5, 1996. I invited Kay, Daniel, Sara, Theresa, Robert and Andrew, and they all came. What has transpired within the group has been a blessing to all concerned and is probably the highlight of the month for each of us. Andrew told me recently that had it not been for the group, he believes he would have killed himself.

Gun on the Floor

Date of Incident: July 1996 Date of Session: July 25, 1996

Note from Constance:

Shortly after our first group meeting, Andrew woke up one morning to find his gun on the floor beside his bed, with no idea how it had gotten there. Needless to say, he was quite disturbed.

Andrew did not write up this session. The following was typed from the notes I took during the hypnotic regression. Andrew speaks slowly while in trance and I was able to write down approximately 85% of what he said.

I gotta get my gun. I don't want to go with them. My gun doesn't work. He's telling me, "That's not necessary. Lay the weapon on the floor," he says. "It's no good to you."

There are two of them, one is extremely wrinkled like he's been soaked in water. The other one is a new one. He tells me I've got to go with him.

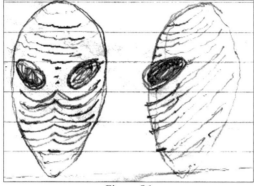

Figure 31

I'm sucked out of my room. What a big craft this is! I go through the roof at a 60 degree angle. It's like a vacuum cleaner. I'm sucked from one point to another. I feel pressure. I'm in a blue tunnel, like the tube for money at a drive-in bank. I see the bottom of the ship.

Inside the ship there are four or five beds, chairs, dentist chairs, and a table that pulls down from the ceiling. I can't have any clothes. They take off my underwear and lay me down on the bed. There's equipment. He's putting one in my mouth. Now he's lifting me up and putting one in my rear end and another around my penis. These are plugged into a machine. I can't feel what he's doing. I ask him why he's doing this and he says that there's still information they need from me. The equipment is some sort of shocking device like a cattle prod. This guy is very different with a pinkish color where the others had a white color. I can see veins, sort of bluish. His eyes are jet black and he is not wearing a uniform. His fingers are real bony looking.

Figure 32

He tells me, "This won't take long. These tests will tell me how much you can stand." The test is to see how much shock my body can take. I go with him. He seems to point at a door and it opens, making a sucking sound. I ask him why there aren't any other people. He says it's not necessary at this point, right now I'm the only one being examined.

Oh! Everything blacked out. I seem to be frozen in this one spot. He's leaving. There's some sort of hurry in the ship. Okay, the lights now come back on. I ask him what happened? He tells me a couple of airplanes got too close and they had to move out, get out of the way. "It didn't take long," he continued, "Only what you call 8,000 miles an hour." I felt nothing.

He's telling me I'm in the control room. There are five other aliens but he tells me, "Don't worry, they won't bother you." I'm interested in the craft. My whole body has been put into their memory banks. He tells me there are two weapons officers. They work independently from everybody else. Their job is to disintegrate, paralyze, and assure their safety. The engine is terrific. It has big blades going clockwise with other things below going counterclockwise. There's a storage room for fuel and other things needed.

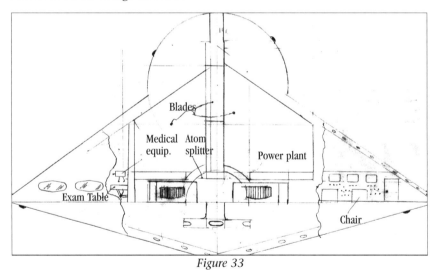

Figure 33

I'm safe as long as I don't touch the cylinders. We enter another room. The wrinkled guy is in this room. I ask how come he's so wrinkled. He tells me if I was 175 years old, I'd be wrinkled too. His IQ would be 275 by our scale, extremely low for their civilization.

I ask what about a place to eat. He tells me, "We don't need food. Our body gives us everything we need from the time we are conceived till we die." He doesn't understand why our bodies need food.

Next we enter a living area. There's a big screen on one wall, chairs, beds, and the glass covered place they rest when they travel.

He tells me to remember the big circle in the control room. It controls everything on the ship: time, atmosphere, etc.

I've got to go back. He puts my underwear back on me. The older person is taking me back. We go through this cylinder. The dog's in the yard but he's not barking. I'm placed right back in my bed. He leaves, and I hear a sucking sound.

I wake up to find my pistol on the floor. I'm wondering how it got out of the sock. That's awful strange, but some parts I can remember.

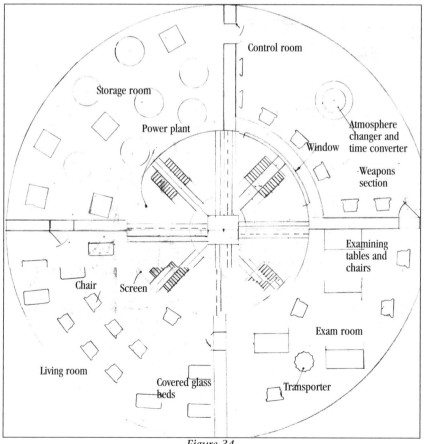

Figure 34

Missing Mole

Date of Incident: October 7, 1997 Date of Session: October 16, 1997

Note from Constance:

In October, Andrew called me to set up a session. He reported awakening to find that his knees were hurting and that he had a rash on his lower body. He had become alarmed when he combed his hair and realized that the large mole on the side of his head was missing. The following is his narrative account written after hypnosis.

❖ ❖ ❖

On October 7, 1996, at approximately 9:30 p.m., I was working in my shop. All of the sudden, I became very sleepy and extremely tired. I was so tired that I could not walk back to my house, which was approximately 10 yards away. I felt that if I could put my head down on the saw table for a few minutes, that I would be okay. As soon as I placed my head down on the saw table, the alien that has always come for me in the past appeared. He seemed to appear through the wall. I knew that I could not fight him like I had in the past. I was simply too tired. He told me that I must go with him. The next thing I knew we passed through the wall and I was in a dome-shaped room.

I was standing in the middle of the room with three Grays around me. I was afraid, but I could not move. One fear was that I would be abducted and not returned. One Gray said not to worry because they had no plans to take me. He stated that other humans had been removed from Earth and that they had not lived. At this time, I felt my body being levitated to a horizontal position and my blue jeans, shorts and shoes were being removed and I was nude.

There were two pieces of equipment in the room. One looked like an iron lung. I was placed in the open area. They placed me so that my navel was slightly above the opening. Body movement or functions of each part of my body were being shown on the screen. During that time, I felt pressure being applied to my lower body. It felt like a blood pressure device.

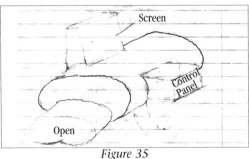

Figure 35

After a period of time, they removed me and placed me on the other piece of equipment that looked like a pair of stairs. My legs were placed into the open area (up to my knees). I was forced to bend over and one of the aliens told me to watch the light in the blue fluid. (I have seen this blue fluid in previous visits). He stated, "If you want to see, you will not take your eyes off the light, no matter where the light moves." As I am looking at the light, I see an object move in my peripheral vision on my right side. The alien warned me, "Don't do that or you will suffer bad headaches."

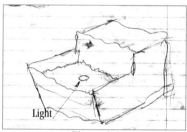

Figure 36

I was removed from the object and my blue jeans and shoes were replaced. My body was being squeezed and I was surrounded by a blue color. The next thing I knew, I was walking with an alien back to my house. We arrived back in my room and poof, the alien was gone. The time on my clock showed 11:30.

The next morning I was combing my hair and I noticed that a mole that I'd had most of my life was gone. It was approximately 1/4 to 3/8 inches in diameter. The mole was located on the right side of my head about one-half inch above the top of my ear and two inches to the back of my ear. Later, when I saw my barber, he noticed that my mole was gone. I told him I'd had it removed. I did this because I can't trust many people.

Also, I suffered with a minor headache all day long. There was a rash around my lower body for two days and I hurt all over for several days. I was bothered with diarrhea and constipation for four weeks.

Note from Constance:

Andrew included the following summary of his psychological symptoms as per my request.

Since I was abducted at the age of six, until now, which covers six abductions, all types of body samples have been taken and many tests have been performed. As a result of these experiences, the following psychological problems have occurred:

I live with frequent flashbacks of the faces of the aliens and the rooms where I've been with them. I have anxiety attacks accompanied by fear of the aliens and what will happen, fear that I will not live, fear of being insane, and fear of being rejected by others. I feel angry, confused, and depressed. As a result, I live with mistrust, self-doubt, and a lack of self worth as I don't always feel able to function on a job.

To combat theses problems, I take Zoloft, Lorzepam, and Alprazolam. I also work with my therapist to relieve the confusion and fear. I knew all along that the life I live isn't really mine to live, because although they usually come at night, these aliens can come at any time and any place.

Quilt Over the Head

Date of Incident: November 27, 1996 Date of Session: November 29, 1996

Note from Constance:

Shortly after the last session, Andrew decided to talk to his minister, with whom he had a fairly close relationship. Instead of being comforted, he was told that these were demons and that if he would tell them that he was a child of God, they would leave him alone.

Seven weeks later, Andrew reported waking up on the floor in the corner of his bedroom, cowering in a fetal position under his quilt. At 1:00 that afternoon, he said he noticed a white scar across his right shin, and showed it to his wife. Within four hours, it was gone. He then called me to make an appointment. Andrew said he had a slight headache and that his hands and legs felt tingly. When he arrived at my office two days later, he was still experiencing numbness in his fingers and legs.

The following are the notes I took during this harrowing session.

I watched Strange Universe and I decided to stay up to watch M.A.S.H. It usually comes on at 12:30. I have difficulty going to sleep. Sometimes I feel sorry for my wife because I stay up so late. Its funny, but like Linus and his blanket, if I can stay up with the TV, it's a comfort. I've already seen M.A.S.H. I turn it off. As soon as I hit the

111

button he's there sitting on the end of my bed. "You know we have to go again." I say, "No, I'm a child of God, I don't have to put up with this." He tells me he's not interested in my religion. What he has to do is more important than my religion. I tell him, "God will surely punish you for this." He tells me, "We don't recognize your God." It's just as well, they may be from that other place.

I'm being squeezed, like a blood pressure machine is being put around me. Again, I'm in this oval room, a place I know so well. I feel like I'm being levitated to a horizontal position. My underwear is being removed. My eyelids are the only thing I can move. I'm floating over to the table. He tells me this won't hurt.

Things are coming down from the ceiling like a milking machine. They are placed on my fingers and something else, a suction cup is placed on the back of my head where the skull connects to the spine. Another set is coming down and three aliens are placing those on my toes. This is gonna hurt! They turn on some sort of power. Power is going through my body, throughout my fingers and toes, but not through the suction cup on the back of my head. It looks like everything is going to a screen with a bunch of lines going up and down, like a heart monitor.

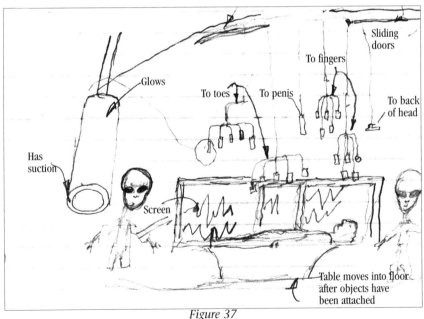

Figure 37

He tells me to be still and not be afraid. I don't like this. They're going to remove the table. I'm just suspended in air. I ask them to release me. They say that they can't, not until they get what they need. I black out. I'm scared. I'm afraid I'm dying. They're letting me hang there like a side of beef. Now they're bringing the table back up. They remove the suction cup from my head, fingers, and toes. Oh, no, they've got another one coming down. I don't want to do that. I don't like where they're putting that one. They're attaching it to my penis. Again the table is being removed. They're putting one on my head again. Again the table comes up. I can feel the table. It's cold, very cold. They're releasing the suction cup from my penis and releasing the suction cup from the back of my head.

He's telling me, "We're finished with the test; that wasn't bad." The bottom part of my body is being raised up. My underwear is being replaced and he tells me they're finished and I'll be returned. I feel squeezing of my body. There's bluish light around me. I'm placed on my bed, but I don't stay there. I get off the bed, crawl in the corner, and put the quilt over my head.

The White Deer

Date of Incident: December 10, 1996 Date of Session: December 12, 1996

Note from Constance:

Less than two weeks later, Andrew called again. He said he had spent the previous day driving to Mexico and back with his son, who lives in the hill country north of San Antonio. He related that what should have been a one hour trip home from his son's house had taken three hours, and the last thing Andrew remembered after dropping his son off, was stopping his truck to look at a large white buck standing in the road! The following are the notes I took during the session.

All of a sudden, the windshield wipers start working and I didn't touch any controls to make these operate. Oh, there's a beautiful deer in the road. It's so white it looks like there's snow on him. I've got to stop. The deer goes off in the brush but my truck won't move. I've got it in gear, but it won't go anywhere.

Oh, I don't like this. Maybe if I push the accelerator... Somebody came along. Oh, no, there's that ship again. I don't like this. It's 100 yards away from me. It looks like it's a phosphorus color. Everything is dark.

They're back again, but they're different. They're different. He tells me he's the same, but he looks different. I ask him why he's different. He says its no concern of mine. His head isn't as sharp at the top. Its more rounded. He's still got the big eyes, but they're further down on his skull. He tells me sometimes we have to do this, meaning they have to change their appearance. He tells me it's no concern of mine.

Everything is just dark. There are no stars or moon, just complete black. There are two of them. He's telling me we've got to leave. I tell him I can't leave the truck in the middle of the road. I want to move my truck. I'm worried someone will hit it but he tells me, "It won't be hit. It can be on the road and not be hit." The pickup is not in my dimension, therefore it can't be hit. Neither can the deer be hit since it's not in my dimension. But I saw the deer. He tells me I don't understand dimensions of sight and non-sight.

They've got a dog on board. He wags his tail when he sees me but when he sees them he backs into the corner, like he's been whipped. He tells me to leave the dog alone. He tells me they're gonna do something to me but he doesn't want me to see it. They try to use dimensions so I can't see it. I tell him I've got to see it. He says, "No, you don't have to see this."

I will see them and the dog, and everything else will be in another dimension. I ask why I can't see it. He tells me, "It's too shocking. We don't want you to see it. I've got to be in this dimension with you. There will be others in the other dimension performing the experiment."

I ask him if they have done the experiment with the dog? "Yes," he tells me. "You don't want to see the experiment with the dog either." I ask him if it will hurt the dog. He tells me, "When you go back, you won't remember. You'll be okay."

I ask about the deer. He tells me, "It was just something to make you stop." I ask if the deer was real. He says, "Do you see it here? What's real is what's here."

I ask if I can touch the dog. He says, "I'd rather you not." In fact, he doesn't want me to touch anything.

I'm fully clothed. I ask him, "In the past you've always removed my clothes, aren't you going to remove them this time?" He says, "Not in this dimension." I ask, "How many dimensions are there?" He says, "How many dimensions do you want there to be?"

I feel sorry for the little dog. He's acting like he's been beat. He's a very shy dog. He asks me, "Are you ready to return to the pickup?" I don't understand that question. I told him if the truth be known, I probably wasn't ready to be here.

I'm interested in what he calls dimensions. I can't get any information from him. I ask him, "Will I be hurting?" He tells me, "Not in this dimension, but in the dimension we put you in, you will be in great pain." I ask him, "Can't you give me something for the pain?" He tells me, "No, it would mess up our test." I ask him if I can see myself in the other dimension and he tells me, "No, it would be too disturbing. What's being done in the other dimension is strictly for our own importance." There's no way I can cross into that dimension. He tells me that I must return to the pickup and the dog must return to where it came from.

I'm back in my pickup and I continue driving down the road. I look at the clock but it's showing the radio station instead of the time. I just want to get out of here. I'm coming into Pipe Creek and no time is showing on the bank clock. I'm traveling back to my house. I'm glad I've got the pickup. I'm bone tired.

Note from Constance:

Once again, we had encountered a psychological block. At first I was relieved, as this version of Andrew's experience was certainly less traumatic for him to re-experience, not to mention, less upsetting to witness. The fact that his recall was blocked bothered him a great deal. A few days after our session, Andrew had a flashback of seeing a section of the ship that was exposed as he was being transported. He drew what he saw (Figure 41) but before we could explore his flashback, Andrew reported another encounter.

The Scratch

Date of Incident: December 27, 1996 Date of Session: January 3, 1997

Note from Constance:

While I was visiting with my family during Christmas, Andrew had a different kind of visit. We met for a session as soon as I returned to town. This time, Andrew said he had been awakened in the middle of the night by a burning pain on his side. Although it had been seven days since the episode, there was a rectangular red raised welt still visible on his skin. The following is Andrew's written account of this hypnotic regression.

115

It is the night of December 27, 1996. I have had trouble with a kidney stone, so I have placed a heating pad on my back. I awaken at 2:00 in the morning and my side is burning. I think that the heating pad has burned me, so I get up and put some Campho-phenique on my side. I think that since it is a burn, I should use aloe-vera on it. I wrap a towel around my waist, and go out on the front porch to pick a piece off of the plant. After applying some aloe vera on my skin, I go back to bed.

All of a sudden, the alien is at the right side of my bed and a light blue circle appears above my bed. It looks to be about four feet in diameter. I have seen this before, and I know that it is the end of the transporter beam. I know that I will be sucked up into this beam, so I grip the sides of my mattress, knowing that at any time I will be sucked out of my bed. The alien tells me that holding the mattress is unnecessary because I have just been returned. Mentally, he continues and tells me not to look into the mirror or television and that my side has been accidentally scratched. He says that they feel bad about the scratch. I tell him he should feel bad about all the other times that they have hurt me and the problems they have caused me. He says those were necessary and that they are not sorry, nor do they feel bad about those. He says that they are willing to let me travel in any dimension that I might choose, except two. I ask how many dimensions there are and he answers with the question, "How many cards in a deck of cards?" I ask, "Why would I want to do this?" He says, "To learn." I feel that he is lying. It could be for them to learn at the expense of pain for me.

The Ink Well

Date of Incident: December 10, 1996 Date of Session: January 9, 1997

Note from Constance:

Six days later, Andrew returned for another session. He reported having flashbacks of pieces of a formula. He asked if he could be hypnotized with his eyes open. He wanted to see if he could write down the formula while in trance. I gave him a pen and a piece of my stationery supported by a book in his lap.

Once in trance, Andrew's hand began to move. From my chair, I couldn't see what he was writing, but I could hear the short jerky strokes of the dried out felt tipped pen as it moved over the textured paper. Five minutes later, he grew still and I began to speak.

The following is the unedited transcript of that session made from a tape recording. The session picks up after I had finished the induction portion of the hypnosis. Freed from the task of taking notes, I became much more verbally active than I had been in previous sessions.

Constance: Tell me what you're feeling.

Andrew: I see the formula, its white on a black background. It comes to me like a tape.

Constance: Like a tape?

Andrew: Like a film strip.

Constance: Like frame by frame?

Andrew: But it's just one constant thing. It's huge.

Constance: Flow of symbols? What do you see?

Andrew: Not much...because it's dark.

Constance: Can you see any of your own body?

Andrew: No, all I can see is just the tape, the math part of it.

Constance: How far is it from you...the white letters or symbols?

Andrew: Maybe a foot.

Constance: It's like you're just looking right at it? Is it at eye level?

Andrew: I feel like I'm looking sort of down on it. Not directly into it.

Constance: Can you tell if you're standing or sitting?

Andrew: I have no...I have no idea of where I'm at or what I'm doing. There's other things. There's gobs of other stuff, just gobs of stuff.

Constance: Again the flow of information?

Andrew: That and it's just...this is the only one that seems to be impressed upon me. The others are...it's hard to say. It feels like I'm in an enclosure, but I can't...it's dark and there's...there must be trillions of things that are in here. Millions. It's so massive. Sort of a cool. I feel sort of cool.

Constance: Certain parts of your body or your whole body?

Andrew: Whole. I feel cool. I can't say it's my body. I don't know what it is. It's like being in a...it's like being in a cave with...you'd think...a good example would be that there would be bats. But the bats are bits of information instead of bats.

Constance: Oh, I see.

Andrew: Something I can associate with because I can think of bats as being maybe millions of bats. There must be millions of bits of information. It's impossible to write all of it down.

Constance: Yeah. You indicate that a certain part is being impressed upon you?

Andrew: A certain formula. It's a certain one. There's...as I said there's other formulas, there's other bits of information. It's not a real good place to be. I'm not...I really don't enjoy being here.

Constance: What's the feeling?

Andrew: It's weird. I don't even know if I can explain it. It doesn't feel like a good place to be.

Constance: Is it a frightening place to be?

Andrew: Well, there's no.... It feels like I've been stripped of all the feelings I have. Stripped of everything.

Constance: Down to some essential component or...?

Andrew: I have no feelings for anything.

Constance: It's disturbing not to have feelings. It's strange.

Andrew: And then on top of it you feel lost. Because you're in such a dark, dark place.

Constance: It's hard to orient yourself at all?

Andrew: There's no orientation. There's...that I can pick up.

Constance: Do you have a sense of when this is occurring?

Andrew: It feels as though I were just dropped into a cave, so to speak.

Constance: Is it a recent experience?

Andrew: I don't know.

Constance: You don't have any idea?

Andrew: I don't know...I don't know what's going on. I feel lost. I feel unimportant. I feel...yet math figures seem to swirl by me, almost faster than I can make out. There's a weird feeling of being hungry...not me but this dark area. I'm not even for sure what I am or who I am or what's even going on.

Constance: Seems unlike anything you have ever experienced?

Andrew: It's just completely weird, a terrible place to be.

Constance: You don't recognize your feelings, your...you don't see your body?

Andrew: No.

Constance: You don't?

Andrew: I have no feelings. Here there's no love. There's no tenderness. It's a bad place to be. It's not painful...I don't feel pain. It's very hard to explain.

Constance: Is it like a place where you cease to exist as the person you know yourself to be?

Andrew: I'm not existing. I don't feel my body.

Constance: Maybe your body is still in that other dimension?

Andrew: I don't feel my body. I don't...it's just complete darkness with...there's circuitry, there's math problems, there's...I mean there's problems that I've never even seen or things that I've never even...it's totally unfamiliar to me. I see circuitry but it's not like any circuitry that I've ever seen before.

Constance: No other presences or figures or...?

Andrew: Nothing.

Constance: Anything you recognize as furniture?

Andrew: Total darkness.

Constance: So the circuitry that you observe is...?

Andrew: Is white on sort of a black background. I'm used to seeing electrical diagrams, electrical symbols, but this has nothing...it's circuitry but nothing like I've ever seen. And it goes on and on and on.

Constance: It seems like a long time?

Andrew: It almost seems endless. It's cool or cold. It's not a good place to be. Again, I just keep looking at the circuitry. It's really...it passes by so fast that I can't really get a picture of it. I can see it but it's just not...I can't write it down. It's moving too fast.

Constance: Too fast...do you get the feeling that this is for your education?

Andrew: No. This is not for my education. It's for their education.

Constance: Is your response to it important to them?

Andrew: I also feel that...they're doing something...it's important to them. I don't know why. Sort of like I'm in a near death experience. I don't see my body. I'm just in...my mind or whatever is just alone in this darkness.

Constance: Can you separate it somehow.

Andrew: As I go through this, it's like a motion picture, but faster. I see things and I try to follow them. And I don't know why this is being done.

Constance: There is a feeling that this is happening?

Andrew: I've never felt that I was just completely in darkness. Some part of me is in complete darkness.

Constance: It felt like when you were so young and taken and placed in a very dark place?

Andrew: This is different.

Constance: This is different?

Andrew: This is totally different.

Constance: Do you remember where you were right before this started happening?

Andrew: Yes. I was in the examination room.

Constance: And what was going on?

Andrew: I was standing there with that other being. I remember back...there was no shadows. I have never seen a shadow.

Constance: When you're there?

Andrew: When I'm there, there is no shadow.

Constance: No shadows...like nobody's body creates a...

Andrew: Uh huh.

Constance: What do you make of that?

Andrew: I don't know. I'm standing with the alien that I know, that usually comes to get me. And then all of a sudden I'm just thrown into a black ink well. There's a fluid because I do feel fluid. There is dampness. There is a liquid.

Constance: Around you...your body?

Andrew: Around whatever I'm in...in this darkness.

Constance: Like you're in liquid?

Andrew: Yes. Whatever part of...I don't have a body...whatever part of me is in this liquid. I would think of it like my mind...like my mind is submerged in the liquid. This liquid is black. I don't see any colors except what appears to be white, I have no feelings. I keep getting told...I must get this information, I must get this information. But it's not, it's just like somebody's telling me but they're not talking. I must get this information. Things must be done. Knowledge must be gathered.

Constance: Gathered for what?

Andrew: I don't know. It just says knowledge must be gathered.

Constance: Gathered by us or by them?

Andrew: By them.

Andrew: Nothing must be left out. I don't like this place.

Constance: It's so strange?

Andrew: I feel...feel weird. It's strange to say that I feel something yet I have no body. I have no arms, yet I feel. It's not...it's not a painful feeling.

Constance: Is this experience happening the night you're coming back from Bandera?

Andrew: I don't know. I just know that my arms, if I do have any...see I'm trying to figure out if I have my arms, my body. I'm trying to picture if I see myself and I don't. Whatever is here is not mine.

Constance: Whatever body, or whatever...

Andrew: It's not mine.

Constance: But your mind?

Andrew: But my mind.

Constance: And your consciousness?

Andrew: As I say, there's no love. There's no hate. There's...it's just a very cold feeling, almost an indifference. I can't...I can't see any part of where I'm at. I just feel...I just feel that I'm not in my body because my mind doesn't have all these outlandish...I don't know if I want to say outlandish or not, but all these math formulas, all these circuits. God, it's amazing. See...when I look at my mind I think of maybe πr^2, but this is way beyond that. And, nothing but formulas, nothing but circuitry. It almost seems endless.

Constance: How does this session, this experience...how does it come to an end?

Andrew: I don't know. It seems endless. It seems like...it seems like eventually...there's other bits of information. There's bits of information that some of it I recognize now.

Constance: Can you give me an example of something you would...you do recognize?

Andrew: Could be πr^2.

Constance: It just goes by and you get it?

Andrew: Which is uh...has to do with the area of a circle.

Constance: Yeah. So some of the formulas are familiar?

Andrew: There's all kinds of information. I see pictures of trees that aren't really trees. They don't look like trees.

Figure 38

123

Andrew: Massive. Massive buildings, massive buildings, not like ours though.

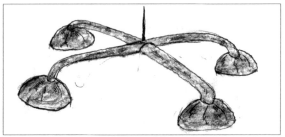

Figure 39

Constance: How are they different?

Andrew: It's like, one looks like a...two bubbles, looks like a bent rod with a half circle, with a big bubble on one end, a big bubble on the other. Then there's another one coming across with a big bubble on its one end and it's going over the other one that has a bubble on the other. Seems to be...there seems to be electrical charges from someplace to another. This is still not a good place to be.

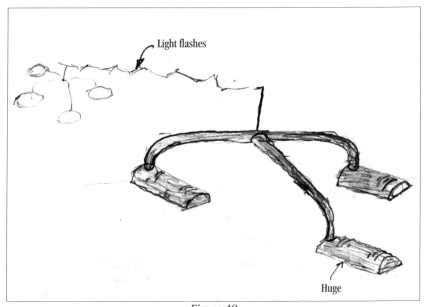

Figure 40

Constance: Do you need to be there any longer?

Andrew: I want to get out.

Constance: Okay. Just let that image fade and see what the next thing that comes to mind is.

Andrew: I'm back in the ship.

Constance: Back in the examining room again...with the same being? Anyone else there or just the two of you, you and him?

Andrew: I think that it's over. While I was there I smelled a very musky...musky, musky smell.

Constance: What's your body aware of? Any sensations in your body?

Andrew: I feel everything now that I'm with the...with him...I just can't move.

Constance: Does he communicate anything to you?

Andrew: No, he was just standing there.

Constance: And then what happens?

Andrew: I'm just standing there with no clothes on. He's telling me that I've got to return to my truck.

Constance: And your truck is where?

Andrew: Bandera

Constance: This is that night?

Andrew: He tells me that he didn't want me to know the whole picture of everything.

Constance: He doesn't want you to know?

Andrew: I have a feeling that I was just sort of fed just maybe a little morsel of what I was taught. I don't know what was taught. He's got me back in my truck again.

Constance: As you are put back in your truck, do you notice anything about the way you are feeling, your body?

Andrew: When I was in the ship, I was extremely numb. The numbness has gone away. I have a feeling that they do this, they paralyze us, because they're really afraid of us. I think they know that if I could have killed them one night, I would.

Constance: Yeah.

Andrew: And in order to stop any aggressiveness, they have to paralyze. That's all. I'm back in my truck.

Constance: Does that satisfy your desire to know?

Andrew: There's more. I have to see. I have to be like...I have to know what went on when I was put into that dark spot. **Something is missing**...I mean I was just popped into this thing.

Constance: Before when you talked of this experience, there seemed to be two beings and a dog?

Andrew: Dog's not here and the other being is not here because there was just total darkness. I think the dog was back where I was, when I didn't have my clothes on.

Constance: So, you know you go from your truck, seeing the white deer. From there, the next thing you know...

Andrew: My windshield wipers start acting crazy first.

Constance: Oh, start going on their own?

Andrew: They start going on their own, they start squirting water on the windshield, windshield wipers start working then I noticed...I noticed the deer. I stop the truck. And then I'm taken out of the truck.

Constance: Do you step out through the door?

Andrew: I go right through the top of the truck.

Constance: And is the engine still running?

Andrew: It is when I get back in. I don't know if it's been running all this time or not. But I know it started...it was running when I get back in. You know, I don't remember if the engine stopped when I went through the top of the truck. The engine is so quiet so it could have been out, but I noticed the panel lights were on, but not the interior, or the dome light. I know that when I push the accelerator the truck moves.

Constance: And as you go through the top of the truck, is that when you saw what you were able to draw? (Refer to Figure 41 which Andrew drew shortly after his missing time in Bandera.)

Andrew: When I get away from the truck a little bit, I'm coming up at about a 45 degree angle from the truck. The beam that they've got me in is not straight down. It's at an angle.

Constance: At an angle, okay.

Andrew: And I'm seeing...I can see the top and bottom of the ship from the angle that I'm in.

Constance: Right.

Andrew: So that the blue light is not straight down, it's at an angle. That's when I see the dome at the top and the panel removed and the ray that they're working on.

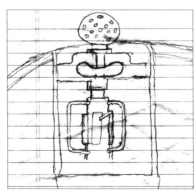

Figure 41

127

Constance: Did you see them working?

Andrew: I didn't see any of the aliens. I just saw that they...that it was open and I assumed that they had been working on it.

Constance: And then as you enter the ship...

Andrew: From the bottom...

Constance: From the bottom? What's the next thing that you recall?

Andrew: I see the huge thing that is coming down. It's like an end of a CO_2 bottle and it's going through what looks to be a crystal or a diamond. That's where the light's coming from. But the light is shining through...it's a diamond turned upside down so that the sharp point is facing to the CO_2 end of the tube and the light is shining down through it.

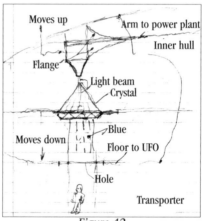

Figure 42

I don't understand how it works. I see the disintegrating ray (Figure 41). It's not in operation. It's just...they've got the cover off. And I saw something like that when I was in that black area.

Constance: Like the ray?

Andrew: Like the parts of it. Evidently they don't need anybody to work on the part that they've got open. I don't know how they're repairing it but I don't see anybody. I don't see any of the aliens. And the next thing I know the...I feel like I'm sort of in a vacuum...I mean

I'm not being moved real fast. But as I move, I feel that I'm being constricted, that things are being, like I'm being squeezed. It's very hard to breathe. The next thing I notice, I'm in the ship and the dog's there and the two aliens are there.

Then the next thing I know I'm...of course he told me that he didn't want me to draw that disintegrating ray. "I'd rather you not draw that." And then the next thing I know I'm sort of being sucked into the dark spot.

Constance: So you're aware of being sucked in?

Andrew: Yeah, I'm aware of being forced in.

Constance: Is it similar to the feeling that you had being transported to the ship?

Andrew: No, not really because I don't feel my body. I can feel my body when I'm going to the ship but in this situation I feel that I'm just being forced in there. Sort of like you take a piece of cotton or something and force it through a hole. A good example would be taking a...putting the cotton back into an aspirin bottle or something like that. It's not painful, but it's not...it doesn't feel like a good place to be.

Constance: If this information, this knowledge is for them, I wonder what would be the purpose of your seeing it?

Andrew: I think they know that I have a desire to know what's happened to me. They don't understand that desire and maybe they're piece by piece giving out information so that the overall picture won't be so shocking.

Constance: Let you know little by little, instead of all at once?

Andrew: All at once, because I think they feel that if I could see the whole picture that I would be very shocked.

Constance: It would just be too much?

Andrew: So they're going to feed it to you like...maybe a piece of candy today, and a piece of candy tomorrow. Sort of getting me conditioned because I think they feel if I have to know this...and see this is the thing that I don't understand because why would they care how I feel? They haven't cared how I felt in the past.

Constance: Right.

Andrew: So, I don't understand...I don't understand what the...why they do this. I've just been abducted many times. I thought I knew these people. I really don't. I don't know anything about them.

Constance: So the better you know them, the less you know?

Andrew: Right. I mean one time I thought I would...I could kill one of them.

Constance: You don't feel that now?

Andrew: Well, I'm getting to feel that somewhere in their feelings or somewhere they have at least a little feeling or they wouldn't scratch me and feel bad about it.

Constance: Right.

Andrew: If they wanted to scare the living daylights out of me, they wouldn't be giving me bits and pieces of information here.

Constance: Or they wouldn't give you any information at all.

Andrew: Right.

Constance: They understand your need to know, or something?

Andrew: So I don't understand. So the more I work with these beings, really the less I understand about them. I know they have no feelings like we have. No nurturing, no love, there's none of that. And I could probably go on and on and on and on as far as the place I was at; I could probably go on and on and on and on because I feel what I saw was just the tip of the iceberg.

Constance: Is it okay with you if it's revealed to you gradually?

Andrew: Well, I've got to know and if it would...I just don't know how I would feel if they all of sudden just dropped this on me. And I'm not for sure they know how I'd feel.

Constance: Uh hum. That makes sense.

Andrew: But again, why do they care? Sometimes I think I see these people caring to some extent. Now I'm not saying caring, like love me or, or...

Constance: That personal...?

Andrew: No, not personal, but this is the part of them that I don't understand. When I first saw them, I thought they were cold and calculating. They don't seem as cold. Maybe something just wears on you.

Constance: You get used to them? Really its amazing that you have been able to access, even on your own, before even coming back to go into trance, you were getting parts of the formula. Remembering. Maybe we have some kind of free will that is honored.

Andrew: But it would be utterly impossible to write down everything I saw. I could write volumes on just what skimmed by me tonight. And some of the stuff, I recognized after a while.

Constance: How about if you just trust your unconscious mind to be able to sift and sort, trusting that you will recall what's most important for you to recall. If there's some reason this formula was impressed upon you?

Andrew: This was the only formula that moved so slow by me...

Constance: So that you could capture it?

Andrew: I could capture it. The others were just flying by like the fast forward on a VCR. And why they slowed down this portion, I don't know.

Constance: Just take a moment to congratulate yourself for doing very good work. Feeling relaxed, renewed and refreshed for having taken the time to do this work. Getting part of the answer that you seek. Maybe not all of it but some of it. You can feel good about that and feel refreshed and renewed. You can return to your normal state of consciousness. Increase the blood flow into your hands, your feet, feeling more and more mentally alert, refreshed, renewed, alert and wide awake.

Note from Constance:

At this point Andrew asked for more paper in order to draw the trees and building he'd seen and I got my first look at the formula he'd recorded while in trance.

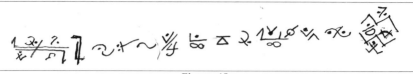

Figure 43

This session marked a turning point for Andrew as he had penetrated part of the memory block. It was a small victory. When I asked Andrew if he wanted to include the drawing of the disintegrating ray (Figure 41) that he'd been discouraged from drawing he said, "Damn right"! But something else began to change in Andrew. A shift in his understanding of these beings was taking place.

The Brain Switch

Date of Incident: December 10, 1996 Date of Session: January 17, 1997

Note from Constance:

When Andrew arrived for his next session eight days later, he related that he was plagued with anxiety and was having frequent flashbacks. He felt there was more to the experience he'd had driving home from Bandera that night than he had recalled. Again, I taped the session. The unedited transcript follows. For those interested in the type of induction I use, refer to Appendix A for the transcript of the initial part of the session.

Constance: What are you aware of?

Andrew: Hurting.

Constance: What do you feel? I want you just to see this on a screen. You don't have to relive it...the physical sensations. Just remove yourself. See the image and see it on a movie screen. You're sitting comfortably, watching. What's that feeling?

Andrew: Being flooded by bright, bright light.

Constance: Is it hurting your eyes?

Andrew: They have my eyes closed. There's something like a gas mask, right over the top part of my head just into my mouth. They've got something on my head. It looks like a cap.

Constance: Is the setting familiar?

Andrew: I'm in the ship, I believe I'm in the examination room. They're experimenting with some type of light, different colored lights. It comes from this machine that goes... The lights seem to come into my mouth. And from that point, it travels all the way down my body. There'll be a red light. It'll travel to my mouth, to my head, and then down my body so that there'll be a red band going down my body.

Constance: Something you can actually see?

Andrew: Yeah, you can see it. Then you see a blue one follow the red. There will be a green, a yellow, all the colors. I don't know what they're doing though. The light is so bright!

Constance: So you can tell the colors, even with your eyes closed?

Andrew: I can see the colors. I'm standing back and...

Constance: And watching?

Andrew: And seeing it. The light is...looks like it is so bright that it would hurt...blind you with light. I'm just laying there with no clothes on. Sometimes they will run another color, the same color again. Like when they run a red, and if they're not...they don't seem satisfied with the red, they'll run it again. And then they'll run a blue again.

Constance: You said all different colors, like there's more than just the red, blue, green, yellow?

Andrew: There's purple, there's brown, there's black, there's lavender, a lot of colors....chartreuse. I don't know what they're doing.

Constance: Is there any sense if this is a part of an encounter that we've already been aware of?

Andrew: I've never seen anything like this.

Constance: Any sense of when this might have happened?

Andrew: I have a feeling that it happened during the Bandera period.

Constance: Who's around you?

Andrew: There's three aliens around me. They're standing behind a protective shield. I don't know why...I don't know why they have to stand behind a protective shield when they've got me exposed! It's a shield that they can see through. Maybe they're not...maybe they're not protecting themselves. Maybe they're seeing things as the light travels down my body.

Constance: Like watching for feedback, or something?

Andrew: Yeah, maybe like...uh, I don't know what it would be like. I can't...maybe like an x-ray, when they're taking an x-ray. They're standing, but they can see...not that they're being exposed to anything...it's that they're...through this picture, this little slot, that they can see through. They can get information about the different colors that are being flashed through my body. He knows this is uncomfortable....that the mouthpiece is uncomfortable. He says that he knows it feels like my jaw is being broken. The piece is so big, sticking in my mouth. He says that he's protecting my eyes so that the light will not damage my eyes. Besides, he doesn't want me to see what is going on anyway.

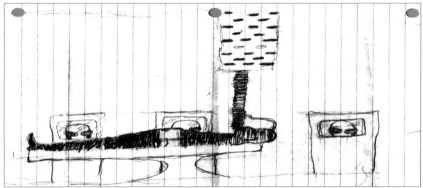
Figure 44

Constance: Is he the same one? The one that came that night in Bandera?

Andrew: Yeah, he's the one that came. And they've got me...I don't understand why but they've got, not only am I...I can't move, but they've got me strapped on top of it. I don't understand why the straps are there. He tells me to be patient...that sometimes they have to run some colors twice, even three times because they need to get additional readings. He says some colors will cause pain, more than others, and that different colors will affect different people differently. Like a red may be very painful to me, but if they run it on somebody else, the red wouldn't be as painful. He says a blue may feel good, but to somebody else, it would hurt. I don't have to have any feelings about this.

Constance: Is this just for information, or is there some benefit to you in having this?

Andrew: No, there's never any benefit to me to have...there's never been any benefit for the person that's been abducted. It seems like the tube is so big that it would be hard for them to get it in my mouth. But the colors start at the tube and they go all the way down to my head, then travel right down my body. If I was guessing, 'cause I don't have my watch, but if I was guessing, it may take ten or fifteen seconds for each color to move down the body. But, I don't know where the color goes after it leaves my feet. It just seems like they can bring the color back in the machine and it goes right on through my body again. They ran the color green about three times. It's sort of funny...it sorta reminds me of lifesavers. They're moving the machine. One of the aliens is...I don't like this. I don't know what they are going to do, and I don't like this. I don't want to do this. I tell one of the aliens that I don't want to do this. Gonna be a brain switch. I don't want to do this. He tells me that I've got to learn to be patient. I tell him, but I don't want to be patient. They're taking my mind or my body and placing it in the alien's. They're doing the same thing for the alien. They're placing it in my body.

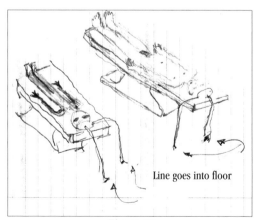

Line goes into floor

Figure 45

Constance: They're switching you with an alien?

Andrew: How cold, how indifferent. Total lack of feeling...any type of feeling. These people...all they're concerned with is information, a massive amount of information. Ah, **this is where I was the other day!** (Referring to the session titled The Ink Well)

Constance: Yeah.

Andrew: All they think about is mathematical and scientific calculations.

Constance: So, the information is inside his mind, or he's looking at it?

Andrew: It's inside his mind. It's sort of like...they don't...their mind's not like ours. It's just weird. Like the formula must be something that is used on the disintegrating ray. I'm sure that the aliens think I'm the one that's quite different.

Constance: Yeah.

Andrew: You see, our minds have mathematical calculations, but our minds cover a large span of stuff, not dealing just with mathematical computations and science, but many other things. What goes on in our daily life...uh...thoughts of our loved ones, in his mind, there's none of this. He's sort of like a soldier. He just obeys orders. Whatever his orders are, that's what he carries out.

They're talking about the colors. The colors are to trace DNA, cell construction, the complete body buildup. And each color has a certain thing that it's to do. I have the feeling that in his mind...it doesn't matter how much pain needs to be created. The important thing is the information. Information is more important than anything else. And see, they don't even care whether they ask you or not. It's not important.

Constance: Do they understand how important it is to us?

Andrew: They don't care. They don't care how important it is to us. That's not what is important. What's important is what they get. It sort of reminds me of a leech. All they're interested in is getting information, whereas with a leech, it's blood, but it would be the same thing. They're just...

Constance: Getting what they need.

Andrew: Getting what they need. And they're not telling me...I don't see in his mind why it's needed. And that's not important to him because everything that's being taken will be studied later on. And that's not...his purpose is strictly to gain information. I think they have somewhat of a feeling that they don't want to purposely cause pain. I don't know if I can explain. I should say, they don't want to deliberately cause pain, but they will not hesitate to get what they want, even if pain is a result. It's like they don't want to hurt people, but if they have to protect themselves, they will. And they won't feel bad about it...they've removed me from his mind now.

Note from Constance:

Andrew was visibly shaken by the brain switch procedure he had recalled. It was the most disturbing of all his experiences to date. Now he knew where he had been while in the ink well. The emotional coldness he had experienced affected him deeply. But this experience also proved to be a turning point as he began to realize that these beings had no malice toward him and he subsequently became less hostile toward them in return.

Missing Kidney Stone

Date of Incident: January 26, 1997 Date of Session: January 31, 1997

Note from Constance:

When Andrew arrived for his next appointment, he reported having more flashbacks. This time, they were of a bubble substance. Once again, Andrew's session was taped and the typed transcript follows minus the induction portion.

Constance: What's going on?

Andrew: He tells me to turn over...that he wants to see my side. I tell him there's nothing there. But he says I've still got to examine your side where the patch was. It seems like he had some concern that it didn't work last time...that it'll have to be done over. That I'll have to go with him.

Constance: Do you understand what he means by "didn't work"?

Andrew: He's talking about the patch.

Constance: The patch didn't do what it was supposed to do?

Andrew: It malfunctioned. He says that I shouldn't worry. There's that tightening feeling again, like I'm being squeezed. I'm back in this room again.

Constance: Is it familiar?

Andrew: Oh yes, I've come here many times. Sometimes I almost feel like it's my second bedroom, I've been here so many times. They're taking my clothes again. They're putting this stuff on me and they put the patch on, to put some gummy stuff on me.

Constance: Where'd they put it?

Andrew: They're putting it all over my body. Some on my legs, some on my stomach, my back, my arms.

Constance: Kind of painting it on or...?

Andrew: Just sort of sticking it on...just sort of looks like putty or gel, that they're just sticking on to me, and it works off the heat from my body. Expands with the heat from the body, sort of a bubble just floating inside.

Constance: What does it feel like?

Andrew: It's weightless. I just feel like a feather. There's no feeling. I feel like I'm floating. He's standing beside me and there's a machine down by his feet. Square and on top there's a bubble. The bubble doesn't fit perfectly with the square. It just fits inside the square. At the end of it, there's...it looks like a telescope, binoculars. They're hooking it up to the patch.

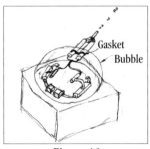

Figure 46

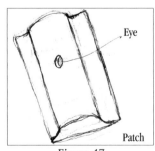

Figure 47

138

Figure 48

It looks like a beam of some type and the beam is going right through the bubble. There's something with the patch...that the beam was contacting the opening of the patch. There's only one of the aliens there, the one that comes to get me. He's the only one there and he's just standing there. I can see what looks like electricity sparking inside the box that's got the plastic dome, or it looks like a plastic dome. I can see electricity, or what looks to be electricity, flashing around going right into the binoculars. And through the binoculars, it's making one point out of the binoculars which is aimed toward the patch. There's a beam coming from that to the patch.

I can't communicate with him at this point. He can't communicate with me. The problem must be that I'm in an enclosed environment.

Constance: I see.

Andrew: He's taking the box away. As he takes the box away, the bubble seems to deflate. My body temperature must change because I thought that the bubble was expanding due to the heat from my body. Another alien comes into the room and he's helping the other one take off this...it looks to be plastic. It just peels off. It doesn't leave any marks. It just peels off. They've got a tube and they put it into the patch. He's telling me what he's doing. They don't make me feel good, at times. I ask what's in the tube and he tells me it's something they want to try in my body. He tells me that it...he's telling me that it can't be detected...that you have to have special instruments. During the time that I was in that bubble, they'd been working with my kidneys. He's telling me that I may have an upset stomach at times. He said that they found something, but they don't know what it is. Evidently they have...feel that they have removed a stone, but they don't know what the purpose of it is. They don't understand why it is in my kidney. He's asking me if it's part of a filtering system. He doesn't understand that our kidney stones cause a great deal of pain, that they're not, uh, something that's necessary for my body. He's asking me if it'll hurt when they remove it. I tell him that it's going to hurt more if he doesn't remove it. He doesn't seem to understand. He's trying to tell me that he thought everything that was in my body was there for a purpose. I keep trying to tell him, no, the kidney stones are not there for a purpose. He wants to know how I got the kidney stone. He's telling me that they're finished with the experiment or the procedure and that I've got to return.

Constance: Do you have a sense of when this is, what night, what...?

Andrew: I just know it was recent. It had to be three or four days ago. But I don't remember this because...I did go to the doctor this week with the pains in my side. But I don't remember when.

Constance: Those are the pains he was telling you that you might have?

Andrew: The upset stomach, sometimes nausea. Because it was like...it won't be so bad that I will throw up, but I just won't feel...feel very good sometimes, and that it might last for a couple of weeks, by our time frame. He's telling me that they work on the stomach through the patch, and they can reform the stomach. And the liquid that they get out of my system, he says it's...he says it's just simple, like y'all having to give birth to a child, you do the same thing with a kidney stone. He's telling me that the kidney may act like it's hurt because the kidney still feels like the stone is there for a while.

Constance: I see.

Andrew: Plus he's still concerned that he's taking something that's vital to me. They're putting on my clothes and he tells me that this time there won't be any markings on my body. If there is any other residue that they've left on my body, once I get back into the atmosphere, the normal atmosphere, then it will deteriorate.

Constance: Is this something that they have done before?

Andrew: They've never done this. The only time they have ever done this...they had a malfunction.

Constance: That's what I mean. Did they try it before and it didn't...?

Andrew: Yes. They tried it before and it didn't work, but they didn't use the bubble. They just put on the patch and it didn't work.

Constance: Is that when you ended up with the scratch?

Andrew: And the...the mark on...

Constance: The mark on your side.

Andrew: Side, what I thought was a burn. They've placed me back in my room, after feeling that squeezing effect which is uncomfortable.

Constance: Are you alone in the room when you get there?

Andrew: I'm alone in my room.

Constance: Do you go right back to sleep, or...?

Andrew: I just go right back to sleep like nothing ever happened. I feel it's just a dream.

Constance: If it weren't for those flashbacks that you've had, you really wouldn't know. And, yet your flashbacks seem to be...pretty...

Andrew: They want me to feel that this is just a dream. I wake up the next morning and I still have pain in my side. I tell my wife that I'm getting tired of the pain in my side...think I'll go see a doctor. Oh, this happened to me Sunday 'cause I'm telling her that I have to make an appointment, on Monday.

Constance: So this would have been Sunday, the 26th?

Andrew: Had to be, because I called the doctor on Monday. It's just another experience of pain and hurt.

Constance: Now, just take a moment to decide if you want to go further, if there's other things you need to know today or if you're content with what you've found. Just take a moment to relax and feel refreshed...renewed. The energy just increasing in your body...a little more alert...fully rested and now wide awake.

Note from Constance:

At last Andrew had derived a benefit from one of his encounters. The kidney stone his doctor had previously confirmed with a sonogram was gone without a trace.

Soon after Andrew's experience, a radiologist was visiting in our home and I had the opportunity to show him Andrew's drawings. He was intrigued with the medical equipment. When he saw the box with the dome that the aliens used to remove the kidney stone, he said, "That's Litho Tripsy." He went on to explain that we have portable and fixed units, which focus an ultra sonic wave to shatter gall stones and kidney stones. He said we've had this technology for about ten years, and that the beam has to be very carefully aimed.

Missing Miles: Second Regression

Date of Incident: June 1,1996 Date of Session: February 20, 1997

Note from Constance:

For several weeks following the above encounter, Andrew experienced a reprieve from the visitors. During this respite, he decided to schedule a session to re-explore his trip to Wheeler. Most of what he wrote following this session was included in the section titled Missing Miles, but the new material that emerged is included here, starting with his realization that his wife had been abducted along with him.

I ask them about my wife. They tell me not to worry. They are running some tests on her. I don't like this because I know what their tests are like, but, I know I can do nothing. I ask where she is. They tell me that there are three dimensions within this room. The first is the room that I am in. The second is the one that has the other individual in it. I tell them she is my wife but they don't understand, we are two separate people to them and not related. Relationships do not exist. The third is a dimension to which I am somewhat connected. At this time, I am still floating and suddenly I feel tingly, effervescent, like an Alka Seltzer. As one part of my body bubbles away, the other part bubbles the body back.

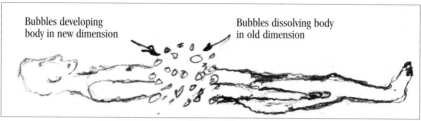

Figure 49

Once I was in this dimension, I saw many compartments pulled out of the wall of the ship. (I had seen the compartments in the wall when I was much younger.) The compartments contained a blue fluid or gas. When this fluid was disturbed, white waves occurred.

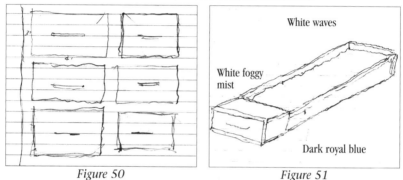

Figure 50   *Figure 51*

Two of the compartments contained human adults (one male and one female). They look to be in their 20's. All of the others contained small half-alien, half-human babies. I was taken to one of the containers and told that it was my child. I was told that it was very ill. The child was very frail. I told them that it is not doing well because it is not getting any affection, no nurturing. I am real mad. "How can you just stick a child in a box? Get the child's mother to nurture it." The aliens said they can't because the child's mother is like them.

They want me to nurture the child and I tell them, "Men don't nurture." I try to explain that only the mother can give the proper nurturing. They still insist. I again try to point out the difference in a father's and a mother's love for a child. At this point, I feel they are lying to me or they are trying to brainwash me.

I stress again the child needs a mother. They ask me if any female would work. I said I guess it would, but you would be lying to that person. They tell me it would be a small thing. I said it would be an unfair, large injustice to that person. I felt that the aliens would do anything to establish their objective.

I look at the baby alien and its head is very large and the body is small. It has a very small mouth. The child's eyes are not as large as the aliens, but they are still too large for the size of the baby. There are no eyelashes or eyebrows. Its nose is very small and seems to be turned up so that the nostrils can be seen. The head is more human shaped than the aliens. Veins can be seen running through its head. The baby's hair stands up like a brush and is very sparse. The eyes do have eyelids. The child has no sex organs, yet they say it is a male. It has five fingers and five toes. Its chin is very small. The child looks to be several months old.

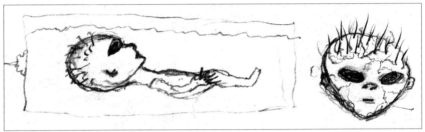

Figure 52

The only thing the aliens know is to keep these babies and humans submerged in this blue fluid with tubes leading to them. I can see that some of these babies are not going to make it. However, they tell me some children are 10-15 years old, according to our time span. They ask me if the other person that I am with could nurture the baby. I said no because I didn't think my wife could handle the problem, since she has many problems of her own, and I didn't think she could handle the looks of the child.

I am being taken back to the previous dimension. After I arrive in that dimension, I ask them to be transferred to the dimension that my wife is in, but I am refused.

Note from Constance:

From this point on, Andrew repeated the same description he had related before of seeing what he thought was a time altering machine and then being placed back in his car.

At the time of this session, Andrew was convinced that the alien was lying to him and that the child he had seen was not his. However, when he returned to talk with me a week later, Andrew was filled with remorse over the fact that he had not nurtured the child. He was also upset to learn that his wife, who he had previously thought had remained in the car during this experience, had been taken as well.

Frozen Shoulder

Date of Incident: March 3, 1997 Date of Session: March 11, 1997

Note from Constance:

Within a few days, Andrew had yet another encounter. When he arrived for his next session, he said he'd been "living off anxiety pills". He related that he had awakened the morning of March 3rd with a red mark under one eye, prompting his wife to ask him if he'd hit himself in the eye. He also had excruciating spasms in his back and shoulder. For seven days, he had been unable to lower his arms which he kept raised above his head, even while under hypnosis. The session was cut short by the fact that he could only sit in a chair for a short period of time. The following are the notes I took during the session.

It's one of my staying up late nights. I had the TV on. That's the last thing I remember. There's a blue light in the room. They're taking me again, but they're not even there this time. It's like in a minute I'm gone. The craft didn't even stop. In the past, the craft has stopped. I'm being taken out of my room. I'm just traveling, but I don't feel the speed.

I'm in that room again and it's the same procedures as always. They remove my clothes. I don't like this. They've got me sort of floating. I'm not on a table or anything. There's a machine that looks like a computer mouse with three buttons.

They put one under my arm and one on my left eye. Both are going to a white screen where there seems to be numbers, or I would guess them to be numbers, or hieroglyphics. It's painful. Even from a distance, I can tell I'm making a face. It must hurt awfully bad.

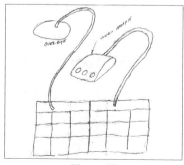

Figure 53

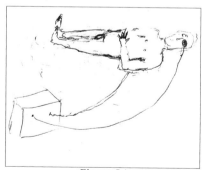

Figure 54

I see him coming with two long needles. He inserts one in my shoulder in between my shoulder blade and neck, and the other beneath my shoulder blade. I think it might be bone marrow that they're after. The needles are removed, but the thing under my arm is still there. It must be sensors, as the screen keeps showing hieroglyphics, three rows of them. Each button regulates different things on that screen.

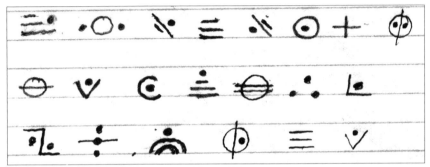

Figure 55

Now the thing on my eye causes me to begin to see different colors: red, green, yellow, and blue. He's beginning to remove the thing from my eye. This is the only test that they'll run at this time. They're going to send me back. Next thing I remember, I'm in my room and I turn off the TV. There were three aliens in the room. I didn't recognize any of them.

Note from Constance:

Following this session, Andrew saw his doctor who gave him a trigger point injection in his neck to relieve his pain. He told Andrew that without the injection he was worried that the shoulder would freeze up permanently. He asked Andrew if he'd been under severe stress. After Andrew's experience with his pastor, he wasn't about to risk telling his doctor what had happened.

Frozen Shoulder: Second Regression

Date of Incident: March 3, 1997 Date of Session: March 28, 1997

Note from Constance:

When Andrew returned two weeks later, his pain had subsided and his face looked more relaxed than I had ever noticed before. He knew there was more to his last encounter than we had uncovered and he wanted to know what else had happened during his two hours of missing time. The following are the notes I took during the session.

146

After I'm on board, I don't see any familiar aliens. I haven't been with this group before. I have the feeling that I'm among strangers. They belong to the same group as those in the examination room. There's a room off to side that looks like aluminum. One of them tells me I have to go in there. There's no door and the windows are not like our glass. It's shiny, brilliant glass.

He'll get me in and back out. He's putting me through the room. I feel different pressures on my cheek, on my back, on the bottom of my feet. It's like a strong, very powerful wind causing the skin to be drawn. They apply the pressure and it goes to every part of my body, they want my side, but not my arm. It's not really painful, but it's not pleasant either. The skin is stretched. Something invisible goes right around my neck and it can apply pressure to every part of the body, even my scrotum. (Andrew is making a face at that point, expressing discomfort).

They're gonna take me back out floating. Now they're doing the procedure of putting those things under my arm and over my left eye. One of them tells me, "You may experience discomfort for a long period of time." It looks like they're taking bone marrow. There's a needle or something in my shoulder.

After this they got something that looks like a wheel that goes on a railroad car, but not as big. There are six of them. I'm being put on top of these wheels and there are also some wheels coming down on top of me. The wheels are rolling on my body. Before, they seemed to be in such a hurry, but now there's no hurry at all. They seem to be testing me like they test our pilots for G's. They want to know how many G's a body can stand.

I haven't seen her before. She's very disappointed that I wasn't willing to work with them. I've been hard to get along with in that I've fought them. She's upset that I wasn't able to help them with the child. I get a strange feeling that she may be the one that is the mother of the child. She's telling me she is the Sectional District Commander. Her name is Zedra. She's telling me I should be very happy as all the tests have been completed, and they won't be needing my services any more. She says, "You should be happy in a way. How does that make you feel?" Out of all the experiences, I've never seen this one before. She's taller, skinnier, and the facial features are somewhat different. She stands about 4'6".

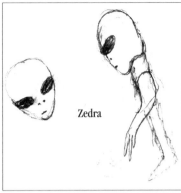

Zedra

Figure 56

I have no hate. I told her that her rank didn't mean a damn thing to me. (Andrew bursts out laughing.) I don't think it pleased her. She tells me most of the females don't have the rank she has, and that most of them take care of the children in the nurseries. She says, "Earthlings are such a pitiful group of people. You can't understand them. In our race, there are no secrets, everyone else knows."

She's disappointed. Throughout the abductions they have every part of me programmed, every nerve, every cell logged in memory banks. I ask her, "Now that you've got all that, you're going to throw me away like an old dish rag?" She says, "There's nothing else. Our needs have been met." Her face is not as long and the top part of her head seems to be larger.

They're not military, not as I know it. Their rank comes from research. They grade things they've done in research. I ask her if there's any other power, someone above her, someone above that person. She tells me that's not really important. Only the things on the ship at the present are important. She could tell me but she doesn't see any benefit in it.

I think she's may be a psychologist or something. She's wanting to know how I feel from the first time I was picked up by them until the present. How do I feel? I tell her "I'm madder than hell." She asks me, "Why are you mad? What is mad? What is hell?"

I told her it's a hostile feeling toward them. I wasn't very happy with all the things they did to me. I ask her why I was chosen? She tells me, they have chosen a group of people from Earth, sort of like "your number was drawn." She says, they didn't intend to cause me harm, only to do what they had to do. She tells me, "If you were in our situation, you would do the same thing, you would do what you have to do."

There's something in her hand and she wanted to give it to me, but its not an instrument or anything like that . She wanted to give it to me, but she's afraid I will tell other people. It feels like I'm being bought. In her hand I see a piece of lead ore or galena. It's two or three inches across and one inch high. It is grey and silver in color. The silver really sparkles, and it has some cleavage to it.

Figure 57

She is holding it out in front of her, and I don't understand why. She tells me, "If we decide to give it to you, you will find it somewhere." She lets me hold it. It's a very heavy mineral. The same mineral occurs on Earth. It is very rare on their planet. With her long fingers, she just takes it out of my hand and puts it on a shelf.

At the time I don't seem to be in any pain. She's asking if I feel sad about being relieved of my obligation. My answer is, "Thank God, I can live my life without their visitations. I don't have to worry about being plucked out of my bed at midnight anymore. At no time has there been a pleasant experience." She tells me she's very sorry for my unpleasant experiences, but there were things they had to do. She's more in tune with my feelings. There's more of an understanding, where the others don't give a darn.

I notice this ship doesn't have containers in it like the other one did. It has an examination table. I don't think this is the same ship. The examination room is all different.

I asked her about my feelings and she tells me feelings are hard for them to understand. She says that feelings cause a lot of problems. I must get dressed and they will return me through the return chamber. I have the same feeling of being squeezed.

Note from Constance:

This was a high point in my work with Andrew. The prospect of an end to his abductions greatly enhanced his prognosis. No wonder he had looked so much more relaxed. His unconscious mind already knew what his conscious mind had just realized...but could he trust them to keep their word?

Documenting Andrew's story has been like building a castle in the sand. To help the reader track Andrew's emotional state, I asked him to write another essay describing his feelings. The following was written right after his meeting with Zedra.

Andrew's Second Essay:

When asked how I feel now, compared to how I first felt when I realized I was being abducted, I would say that I am very fortunate. Even though my abductions were straight out of hell and my days and nights were almost impossible to live with, I have had a wonderful social worker and a great abduction group to help me. Without their help I probably would have gone crazy or committed suicide due to the following problems.

No one would have believed me. I lived with panic attacks and the fear of hellish abductions that could occur at any time. It is a great help to hear that others have these problems and that I am not alone. I am grateful to my wife who gave her support, and to the people in the group who helped me to work out and live with the alien abductions that robbed me of my childhood and most of my adult life.

I don't want anyone to believe that everything will be roses in the future. Even if the abductions stop, I will never be the same. Nightmares will always be a possibility, along with panic attacks. I will probably have to take medicine the rest of my life.

I would like to say that I have written this for other abductees. To let them know that there is help and that there are others that have gone through the hellish abductions. If you are an abductee and need help, visit a UFO organization and find out if there is an abductee group in your area. Ask if there is a social worker that works with abductees or write to another abductee.

Nose Bleed

Date of Incident: April 7, 1997 Date of Session: April 11, 1997

Note from Constance:

For more than a month, Andrew was left alone, but on April 7th he reported waking up at three o'clock in the morning with a nose bleed. For the next two nights he had nightmares of being cut and healing without bleeding. He was also plagued by a particularly disturbing flashback of a piercing eye that seemed to be almost touching his.

When he saw me four days later, Andrew said he had been having headaches that lasted all day. Once again, the regression is documented by my notes of the session.

❖ ❖ ❖

My room is sort of a bluish color. Two aliens appear in my room. One is at my bedside. The other one's by the door. That's strange. There's a clothes hanger on the door. He's not on the floor, but he's elevated himself and the clothes hanger looks like it's sticking right through him.

The one by my bed is the one that's always accompanied me to the ship. He knows the promise that was made, but I have something of theirs and they've got to get it back. They forgot it and they can't let me go with their property.

They have got to take me back to the ship. The next thing I know I feel like I'm in a vacuum cleaner, being sucked out of our room, so to speak. Both of the aliens are being sucked out of the room. The color just seems to suck back into itself.

They do the same thing that they normally do. They always take my clothes off. I only have my underwear on. I'm being placed on the table. It looks like the woman alien is pulling the machine down. It looks like a spark plug. It's being placed in my nose, in each nostril. They do one side, and then they do the other. She's telling the others to turn me over on my stomach. When they put that thing in my nose it's very cold. It hurts very bad from the look on my face. When they turn me over, I feel the same coldness behind my knee, then behind the other knee, and again it's very painful. Again they turn me over and she tells me to relax and lie there for awhile.

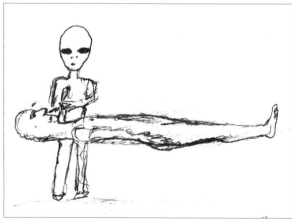

Figure 58   Figure 59

In a very short time, one alien is putting my underwear back on and he's saying " I've got to remember that this slit goes in front." They're standing me up. I still can't move, but they're taking me over to this sort of door. It's in the floor, and seems to be a door. Again I feel this sucking sensation, but this time only one alien goes with me. One of them stays there. I'm back in my room. This is strange...he takes his finger and puts it on my head and moves it all the way down to my feet. At this time I feel like I can move.

He said they had to do this, but they couldn't let me go with their property. Since I have already told people about them, they're concerned that someone may try to extract their property from my body. He's telling me that I could have headaches, nose bleeds, that my legs could ache, and my stomach could be upset. He says not to worry because this will pass. He says he must go and the next thing I notice is that everything is being sucked up out of the room. It's like all the color is being vacuumed. I must have gone to sleep because I don't remember anything else. I've never seen the transportation work like that. I wonder if they developed a new transport method - the color seems to be sucked up with it.

Note from Constance:

Andrew returned to my office the evening of this session for our monthly support group meeting. Toward the end of the group, Robert noticed that Andrew's tremor was gone from his hands. This was amazing, as Andrew's hands had shaken all the years I had known him. But that night, as he held his hands out for all of us to see; they were rock steady. Andrew said he felt better than he had felt in his whole life and that he was able to think much more clearly than before.

For eleven days Andrew enjoyed his new found energy and clarity. For the first time he could remember, he was free of the "sinking spells" that he normally experienced in the evenings. Having his implants removed definitely agreed with him. He said that he wanted to continue seeing me twice a month in hopes that he could lessen his residual anxiety and find answers to some remaining questions.

Men in Black

Date of Incident: April 22, 1997 Date of Session: April 22, 1997

Note from Constance:

When Andrew called for his next appointment he said he wanted to explore a dream. He did not mention on the phone that he had drawn two pictures from his last experience (Figures 58 & 59) and was bringing them to me along with copies of a handout on panic attacks that he had reproduced for the group. While making copies of the handout, Andrew made copies of his two drawings as well. This was a stroke of luck as the originals were about to be taken from him.

The morning of his appointment Andrew awoke to find a piece of lead ore (galena) sitting on his dresser. It was the same one Zedra let him hold during his March 3rd encounter, the one she had told him that he would "find somewhere if they decided to give it to him." Andrew picked it up and without telling anyone, he put it in the front seat of his truck along with the papers he was bringing to me.

I knew something was terribly wrong the moment I greeted Andrew in the waiting room. I had never seen him so upset and angry. My office is upstairs and it is my custom to accompany my clients from the downstairs waiting room up the stairs to my office. Some clients make small talk during this passage while others remain silent until they are in my office with the door closed. Never before had Andrew started talking to me on the way up the stairs, but this day he was furious and he couldn't contain himself.

Once again our hopes of a peaceful end to Andrew's ongoing nightmare were dashed, but this time it wasn't the aliens who had betrayed him. It was worse. As I listened to his story, I noticed that his hands were again trembling and I felt a shudder go through me.

The following is the account he later wrote describing what happened to him on his way to my office that morning.

On April 22, 1997, at approximately 9:15, I am driving east on Loop 410. My speed is 60 mph. I am going to an appointment which is scheduled for 10:30. I look in my rear view mirror and see a black 1996 Chevrolet Lumina approaching me with a red light flashing on its dash. I'm thinking that it is an unmarked police car, so I pull off 410 onto the shoulder. I see two tall men get out of the car. Both are dressed in black suits, sun glasses and hats. I think that they may be detectives.

I roll down the window of my pickup and ask them what I did wrong. I am told, " Get out of the truck now." He has a rough, gravelly voice (Figure 60). As I do, the other one picks up the alien gift and some pictures I have drawn. Hurriedly, he looks at them and keeps the alien gift and two drawings and throws the other papers out on 410. He also takes the keys and throws them under the tool box of my pickup. As this is being done, I tell them that they can't do this. That is my property and that I am an American citizen, which means I have rights.

As I say this, I look at the car. There are no tags on the bumper and no stickers on the windshield and I notice a third man in the back seat. The man (#1) tells me that I have no property except what I was born with and even that is questionable. "It's nice that you are an American citizen, but that doesn't mean much in this case. You are expendable."

I tell them that I will report them to the police. He tells me, "Go ahead, make out a false police report. We don't exist according to your government. No one will believe you and you will only make it hard for yourself."

They get back in the car and leave. I am thinking I should follow them, by the time I get my keys from under the tool box in the back of the pickup cab, they are gone. So I pick up the papers that they threw on the freeway and drive on to my appointment.

At this point, I am burning mad and shaking uncontrollably. I am thinking what would they want with some lead ore and some sketches? I know lead ore, as geology was one of my minors in college and this one looked to be 100% lead. Somehow, someway, was something encased in it? But why were the sketches taken?

Note from Constance:

After talking for an hour Andrew was finally calm enough to go under hypnosis and we were able to investigate the dream he had wanted to explore. My notes from that regression are included in the section titled The Big Book. Before bringing him out of hypnosis, I had Andrew re-experience his encounter with the Men in Black. The following are the notes I took as he described these men.

The one talking to me is wearing black, sharp-toed, cowboy boots. His ears are close to the head. Both of them are wearing light-shaded sunglasses. I'm somewhat amazed at the gloves. They're black latex or Playtex. I can't see through them. I don't detect a bulge of rings or watches beneath the gloves. They don't want any fingerprints left.

They are wearing breast type suits with vests, black shirts, black ties, and identical glasses. Their hats are black. They're not western hats, but are short brimmed and creased at the top with black feathers. There are no other colors. Even the stitching around their boots is black. One of the men seems capable of growing a heavy beard. The other one would have a regular beard. There are no scars. They would be approximately 35-40 years old.

Only one speaks. He has a gravelly rough voice, one I wouldn't forget. It's quite different from any voice I've ever heard. It's a voice that would stick in your memory. He has no mustache. Both of their coats have a slit in the back. I think what they're wearing would be very hot, but they're not sweating at all. They remove the light from the dashboard of the car when they leave. The car is totally black except for the red light

The height of the one talking to me is 6'1". He has no beard at all. His face is egg-shaped. He has a very pronounced groove under his nose. These men don't smile. They're very solemn. When the one man says I'm expendable, he's not just talking about me, he's talking about my wife, my son, and anybody else I deal with. He makes me feel like I've been a very bad boy. These men have got a certain power. I think they could be very ruthless if they wanted to be.

They don't ask to look in the tool kit, nor do they take the keys and look in the tool kit. They're after certain things and since they were on the seat, that's what they found and they didn't look any further. They can see what they're looking for. They know exactly where things are that they're looking for.

I just feel very strange around them. I feel they're human but there's a very unsettling feeling. You don't want to piss these people off. Just do as they say and don't fight them. When I was with these people, I was more afraid than when I was with the aliens.

Note from Constance:

After Andrew came out of trance, he told me that he wanted to tell me the man who threw his papers out in the freeway, "Hey, you don't have to litter," but he stopped himself. Seeing as how Andrew has never held his tongue with his alien captors, I realized he must have been very intimated by the men in black...but not too intimidated to draw their pictures for the book.

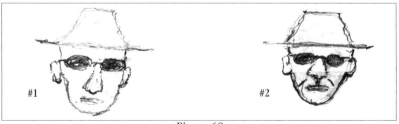

Figure 60

155

Whitley Strieber has told me that he considers therapists who are willing to work with abductees to be "front line soldiers" and that I can call upon him any time I need help. This was definitely one of those times. I was leaving town the day after this session and would be gone for a week. I was rattled by this latest development in Andrew's life. Alien abduction was bad enough, but to be harassed and threatened by fellow humans simply because you are an abductee is unforgivable. Hadn't Andrew been through enough?

I placed a call to Whitley and he called me back at midnight. I didn't get much sleep that night, but I felt better after talking with him. In short, Whitley theorized that the 'Men in Black' could be an 'unsanctioned military group' of some sort.

Whitley advised that Andrew make out a police report. He said that if the police had received other reports, they would be very interested. I related this information to Andrew, and while I was away in California, Andrew did attempt to file a police report. He said that the policeman who came to his house seemed interested in taking his report until he mentioned that the two men who had stopped him were dressed in black. At that point, he said the policeman stepped back explaining and said that he was going to save him from making a false report, and he left.

Several days later, I received this note from Andrew:

About a week ago, I came home, opened the front door and removed the keys. I then shut the door but did not lock it. I put up the articles I bought and went to lie down. Later I went to find my keys. No keys - nowhere. I turned the house upside down - still no keys and no keys up to this date. Is this connected?

After that, things were quiet for a few weeks, until Andrew received a threatening letter in the mail "advising" him to drop out of the group, withdraw his story from the book, destroy his sketches, and stop talking about his experience. The letter was unsigned and though Andrew said the postal investigator did everything he could to trace it, the author could not be identified.

For awhile I watched my rear view mirror and hid copies of Andrew's drawings in obscure places. I wondered how far these men would go to achieve their aim?

Robert later told the group that he had found out from his friend who works for the C.I.A., that these guys are referred to as "The Spider Men". They are ex Navy Seals, and other Special Forces who carry out their assignments with no questions asked.

Fear is an insidious thing and if you give it room in your life, it will consume everything in its path. After a few weeks of worrying, I decided that whoever these people were, there was one thing I could conclude about them. They were cowards! Ultimately I decided that anyone who wouldn't show their faces or sign their names didn't deserve any more of my energy. Their efforts to intimidate Andrew, only increased his stubborn determination, and fueled my resolve to complete this project.

The Big Book

Date of Dream: April 19, 1997 Date of Session: April 22, 1997

Here is a summary of the notes I took during the session involving Andrew's dream. I don't know if this was a dream or if it was an encounter, as no information emerged about being taken or returned.

A big fan is blowing the pages of a book. The alien is pointing to the pictures. (Andrew begins to describe the images found on each page and they are images from his encounters going back to 1942. It seems as though everything he has seen is depicted on the pages of this book.) The alien points at each one as they fly by, pointing them out individually. It's like a photograph book. It's very unsettling. His bony fingers point to them. They are not in the sequence that they happened. Like there is a picture of the alien going through the tent from the outside, and a few pages over, there's an inside picture of the tent. I can see the boy scout yelling. His mouth is open, but there's no sound. There's equipment, a bear claw, the thing that went up my penis. (Andrew lists more images.) I see myself being taken on board the ship. Most pictures are things I've seen, like the instrument they took my implants out with. I see all the children from my first abduction, some Black, some Mexican, some Indian, some White. I see the faces of the children, the horror, like they're frozen, scared to death. There's a picture of my grandparents' house. Pictures of when I've been tested for feelings regarding things that happen on Earth.

One book is closed and another is being opened. (Andrew mentions more images.) I was told not to go any further. All the pictures seem to have depth to them, like 3D pictures. Cyan seems to stand out of the book. There's the half faces that I thought was a dream before, half faces, being half alien, half human. There are children taken out of the cabinet and there are children in water.

The finger that is pointing to the pages seems to have just touched the picture with his finger and the water changes, making waves. He can reach into any picture with his finger. He seemed to want me to remember the water as making white waves. There's a picture of brain transference and a picture of me at boy scout camp.

He comes to the end of the book. His hand is withdrawn and I'm left in darkness. Something is missing. A picture is missing. There is no end except when the cover is closed. There is room for more pictures.

The Merry-Go-Round

Date of Incident: Spring 1996 Date of Session: May 6, 1997

Note from Constance:

Denial is a funny thing, and therapists are not immune to it. During the spring of 1996 Andrew reported a disturbing dream. He was left with images of half human, half alien faces. Though he drew pictures of the faces at the time, neither he nor I suggested he explore his dream to see if it was an encounter.

Figure 61

A year later, Andrew came across a book with a cover bearing an image similar to the ones he had drawn. The following are the notes I took during the session we had to explore his dream images. Now I understand why he avoided this material for so long, as it turned out to be the most disturbing of his experiences to date.

I'm in the dark. A light turns on. The only light is shining down on me. Two aliens come out of the darkness. I can't move. I have no clothes on at all. One alien is picking up my hand and my arm. He seems to be working with my joints, bending my finger down. He's puzzled because my joints don't work like he thinks they ought to.

He's bending my fingers back the wrong way. I tell him, "You son of a bitch, it doesn't work that way."

I get tired of these things. They act so stupid sometimes. He wants to record the feeling I have when one sperm comes out. He's trying to get me to work with him. He wants me in a certain mood where I'll cooperate with him. "You son of a bitch, I'm not going to cooperate with you at all."

He tells me they can make me do that. He tells me they can do away with all my resistance. It's like inducing a dream. His eyes are coming very close to me. Once his eye gets close, they can almost make you do anything they want. I'm on some sort of a moving belt. I'm tied down. They're going to run me through a saw mill if I don't do what he wants. I'll feel every pain. I will go through it as if I were run through a saw mill.

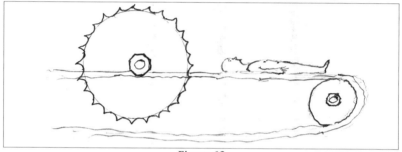

Figure 62

You don't have any resistance. You've just got to go along with him. He's sitting me up on a table. His bony fingers move up and down my spine. Oh! Four more lights turn on. Oh, oh! There's a merry go round. Oh! Instead of horses, there are individuals. They are half human and half alien. I don't understand this! They're just moving around in a circle. They act like they're drugged. I read the mind of one of the humans.

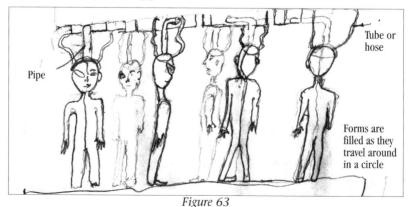

Tube or hose

Pipe

Forms are filled as they travel around in a circle

Figure 63

He's saying, "Don't let them do this to you!" I ask what they're doing. "They're connecting our DNA with theirs," he communicates to me. I move my head and I can see a glass tube with metal at the top and metal at the bottom. Inside, there is a human (Figure 64). He's in great pain!

"You stupid S.O.B., you've ruined this human's life." He tells me, "Don't worry about it. It's our business. It's a minor thing. We hope to get more information." I tell him it's wrong to do this. He says, "Wrong? Who are you to tell us it's wrong?" They had permission of the alien to do this. I ask him, "What about the human?" "It isn't necessary."

I see another tube, a larger tube. It's two tubes put together. There's nothing in it. At the top of each tube, there is a line or hose going over to a box. The box is attached to the ceiling.

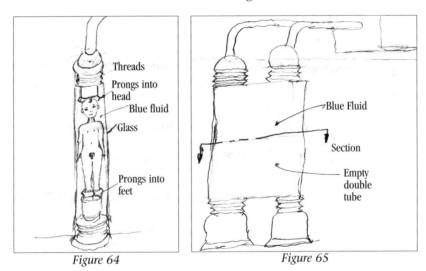

Figure 64   Figure 65

He's telling me, "You're a little bit out of sorts today." I tell him, "That's an understatement. I'm just madder than hell!" He wants to return me to where they picked me up. Maybe I'll feel better for future tests.

I ask him, "Why do you keep doing this? Why not do it all at one time?" He tells me there are many people involved in this. When information is fed to certain ones, that's the one they have to go get. I tell him, "Keep the hell out of my life." He tells me, "We can't do that." I reply, "I don't understand why you keep doing this." He tells me, "Don't you know that you are the chosen people. You are the chosen one. Do you know you've been asking that question for fifty-four years and we have refused to answer your question, 'Why me?'"

I don't like this. I think he's lying to me. He's trying to brainwash me. I don't want any part of this. He tells me that I was the chosen one at birth and all this information had to be accumulated. He tells me in 1957 I had a major operation. They knew about it. He's tells me, "You wouldn't have died. We wouldn't have allowed it." I tell him he had nothing to do with that. My girlfriend pulled me through. He says, "You really don't know, do you?"

He's trying to brainwash me. I have but a few more tests to be run and they will have completed everything that they needed. At that time they will leave me and they will not return until I pass away. "Upon your human death, you will become one with us." I tell him, "No way." He's trying to brainwash me again. I'm telling him my Bible doesn't say that. He tells me, "Believe what you want to believe, but we know the truth." It's a damn lie. I don't believe him, yet he tells me he doesn't really care what I believe. "Why do you think we've worked all this time with you?" I refuse to believe it.

He's telling me they will put on my clothes (just my underwear) and I will be returned. They will come back because they have several groups of tests they have to perform. They don't know when. It's not up to him to decide. It's like being a soldier on Earth, you receive your orders. It's the same way with him. I don't have a choice and he doesn't have a choice.

"It's easier on you if you'd just relax." "Relax, hell, when you tell me things like this, how am I supposed to relax?" He's telling the other alien to return me to where I was picked up. Everything goes black and I don't hear anything. There is a musky smell.

Note from Constance:

Never before had I heard Andrew swear as he had during this session. I don't know what upset him more, seeing what was happening to the humans or being told he would become one with the aliens upon his human death. Although some abductees like Kay and Lydia might find this to be a comforting thought, Andrew was horrified by the idea and refused to believe it. He even talked with me about deleting that part from the book as he feared it might be too upsetting to others. Ultimately Andrew decided it was best to include the whole story, like it or not.

Benji

Date of Incident: June 12, 1997 Date of Session: June 19, 1997

Note from Constance:

As far as Andrew knew, he had not had any alien activity since his implant removal on April 11th. We had met twice since his last hypnotic session, and were able to talk for a change. However, on June 12th, Andrew became suspicious. He had been awakened at 3:00 in the morning by his dog, Benji, who was growling and barking from under the bed. He had the feeling that there was a stranger in the room. Under hypnosis, the following encounter emerged as documented later by Andrew.

❖ ❖ ❖

Benji, my dog, is growling and barking from under my bed. This is very unusual because he only barks when someone is around that he doesn't know. He only tolerates about four people. He does not like my own son.

The bed that I am sleeping in is a double bed and I keep a .38 pistol under the mattress. The light in the hall is on. That helps us find our way to the restroom. The light in the hall, is shining into my room. I see a humanoid with its back toward me. I get very mad, because I think it's the Grays. They had promised to leave me alone and I expected them to keep that promise.

I reach for my pistol. The alien turns and I see that he is not a Gray. He mentally tells me "Andrew, I will not hurt you," and he tells me to put down the gun. At this point, the bottom portion of my body feels effervescent and I notice that the alien is also disappearing from the bottom up. I do not hear Benji barking any more.

The next thing I know, I find myself outside. It is hot, sticky, and humid. This is odd because I do not see my body. We are headed toward the creek. This creek is part of a drainage system and has a bed of concrete with concrete sides of 45 degrees. I do not see any other man-made objects, such as lights.

At this point, I see a ship. The top turns bluish white. The ship seems to pulsate. The bottom of the ship is phosphorescent. There are four recessed windows. Looking at the ship, I would guess it to be 50' in diameter and 10-12' high. The ship is hard to see when it turns whitish-blue because it blends with the concrete. The alien tells me mentally to enter under the bottom of the ship. During this time, I have not felt any squeezing as I felt with the Grays. We enter the ship and he tells me to sit in the chair which is located approximately in the center of the room. I am very hesitant in response to his order.

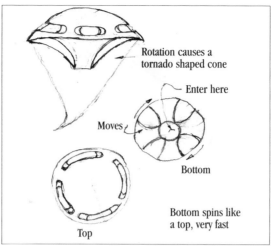

Figure 66

He asks, "Why do you hesitate in following my command?" I tell him that I have two reasons. First, that I do not trust him, and second, I don't know if I can sit in a chair without a body. Again, he reassures me that he will not hurt or harm me in any way, and then he asks me how I know I can't sit down if I have never tried it.

I go to the chair and sit down and as I do, my body starts to materialize along with his. This starts from the head down and I feel a bubbling effect again. I ask him if my clothes should be removed and he tells me that it's not necessary.

To my right, there looks to be a huge TV screen with buttons or lights of different colors. There is also an object that looks like a TV dish. The chair reminds me of a dentist's chair. He has also materialized again at this point, from the head down. He is the only other being in the room. The object that looks like a TV dish begins to move, and it shows pictures of my brain. Sometimes the brain revolves. There are other pictures of my brain shown in many sections.

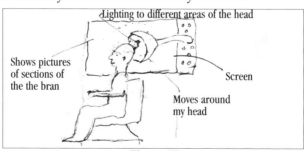

Figure 67

The being moves to the other side of the room and brings back two hand-held objects. He takes one instrument and begins to move it over every millimeter of my head. As he does this, I hear beeping sounds. Sometimes there is only one beep, at other times there are many beeps. When this happens, he takes the other instrument to remove the many beeps. These beeps also show up on the screen in the brain.

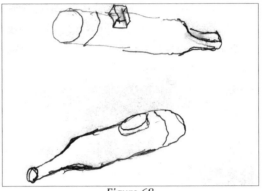

Figure 68

Again, I tense up and again he assures me that he will not hurt me. I ask him, "What are you doing?" He tells me he is removing memories of the Grays. I ask him, "What if I do not want them removed?" He tells me that he can't understand why anyone would want to keep such terrible memories. After he has gone over all of my head, he tells me that it is time to return. Again, I feel a bubbling feeling from my feet up. I also notice that the being is doing the same. We go back out of the bottom of the ship and we go back to my house. He stops outside of my house and tells me that he must leave because he has lots of work to do.

The next thing I know, I am back in my room again feeling the bubbling effect. When I wake up in the morning, I feel a hard object in my bed. It's the .38 pistol. I hear a noise. The sound is a thump, thump. I look on the floor next to my bed and it's my dog, Benji, wanting to go for his morning walk. I asked my wife if she heard Benji carrying on so bad last night and she said that she had not heard anything at all.

Note from Constance:

After coming out of trance, Andrew described the ship he had seen as hovering over the ditch as though it was designed to fit there. Here is Andrew's description and drawing of the alien, which he produced shortly after the session.

The creature looks like a Vietnamese skull with a helmet from the front view. He has no nose, a small mouth, and no ears. The top of his head has small wrinkles with bluish veins. Other than that, the skull is pinkish-gray and is translucent. His eyes are slanted, large, and black. From the side view, his chin is sharp and his helmet now looks like a cap. It seems to curve up and return to his skull.

His body is covered with a tight suit with no buttons. He has broad shoulders with a small waist. His body is long with long arms. He has four long fingers, and his thumbs are short stubs. His feet are in boots. He has no fingernails.

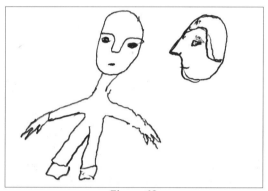

Figure 69

For once, Andrew was actually pleased to have had an encounter. His flashbacks had been driving him mad. One morning in church he had looked at the minister and had seen an alien standing in the pulpit. The entire background had disappeared and only the alien was visible. Needless to say, this had been most disconcerting. Now Andrew was hopeful that the flashbacks would stop. He asked to see me again in two weeks to find out whether his memory of his experiences had really been erased.

Session Notes: July 3, 1997

Andrew started this session by stating that he felt great. His skin color was good and he looked rested. He related that he had been completely free of flashbacks since our last appointment and that he was sleeping well as he no longer felt reluctant to go to bed. He said that he was finally able to focus on the things that were important to him. When I asked what those things were, he answered, "my wife, my dog, my shop, staying busy". At last he was enjoying his life.

As we talked, it became clear to me that Andrew truly did not remember his experiences. I guess I had hoped this was just another memory block and that his memories would be safely tucked away, but he was unable to retrieve anything under hypnosis. Even things that he had previously consciously remembered, like the white deer and the missing miles were gone.

Andrew had told me that he kept his drawings and accounts in three brown envelopes. Under hypnosis, I asked him to go into his files and tell me what was there. He said, "All I find is blank paper...sheet after sheet of blank paper." He did however, remember his last experience and he did remember the squeezing sensation that he had always felt when being transported by the Grays.

Note from Constance:

Neither Andrew nor I knew what to think about this turn of events. Though he felt tremendous relief, he also expressed a feeling that surprised me. Like the young man in the movie *Ordinary People* who held on to the boat as his brother drowned, Andrew was experiencing survival guilt. Why had he been spared by this benevolent being and others in the group had not?

He called me that evening to say he didn't know how he would feel with the group, which was meeting that weekend to review their stories and sign releases. Somehow, he no longer felt the same bond he had felt before. Again he expressed his desire to help others and I assured him that by sharing his story, he had already done his work and that he could continue to help others just by being open to them.

The problem that remained was mine. In order for Andrew's story to be included in the book, it would be necessary for him to read it before signing a release. Andrew and I discussed how reading his accounts might affect him. Would it be like reading something for the first time? Would his memories return? What about his traumatic feelings? Would they return as well, or would it be like reading something that happened to someone else? Could he have his memories without the traumatic feelings? I didn't know what to expect.

From a therapeutic perspective, I was in a bind. I wanted to do what was best for my client. Philosophically, the idea of taking a person's memories away bothered me, as I believe that our responses to our experiences shape and define us as individuals. However, people who have been brutalized often identify with the aggressor and reenact the trauma creating new victims. Considered from that perspective, the ability to erase the memories and the traumatic feelings could be extremely beneficial. In any event, I couldn't argue with the fact that Andrew's psychological condition was vastly improved, although only time would tell for how long.

Not knowing what would be best for Andrew, I left the choice to him. He could leave well enough alone and withdraw his story from the book, or he could read his story and risk the return of his anxiety symptoms. Andrew told me that he had already given me permission to tell his story and that he would not take it back. Bottom line, he wanted to help others.

Andrew wrote the following essay shortly after meeting with the group on July 12, 1997.

Andrew's Third Essay

I have been in therapy for over a year. When I first started, I was a real basket case. My hands shook constantly and I had trouble speaking. My mental health was very poor. Panic and anxiety attacks were very common. I feared I was going insane. My therapist helped me by working out my abduction problems, while my group worked to show me that I wasn't the only one.

As for the results of the last alien's visit, it's simply too early to know. I cannot begin to tell you how much help a good therapist and abduction group has been to me. Maybe one of them should write up the difference they see in me. I only know that my panic and anxiety attacks are gone. My speaking has improved and I have lost the feeling of being insane. I can truly say my abduction group is my support family.

After meeting with the group on Saturday, July 12, 1997, I have found out that if I read one of my abduction accounts, it does come back, but there is no feeling of trauma. Could it be that the last being could not remove the trauma without taking the memory as well? In doing so, the trauma has been blocked and I am free to let the memory come back if I choose to do so.

Note from Constance:

If treating Andrew doesn't turn out to be *The Case Study* of my professional career, I can't imagine what else is in store for me. In all my years as a psychotherapist, I have never before witnessed the spontaneous remission of a client's anxiety disorder. Andrew appeared calm and relaxed and his formerly pale complexion had been replaced by a rich skin tone. All I can say is, it's truly amazing!

The Check-Up

Date of Dream: September 6, 1997

I have just awakened from what I thought was a dream and I tell myself I must write this down. I dream I am in bed and I open my eyes. I see the alien that visited me the last time standing by my bed. Mentally he tells me that he has arrived "for my check-up". Again, in his conversation, he uses my first name, "Andrew". At this time, I find myself afraid of him, mainly because of his appearance. I try to get out of bed, but it's of no use. My arms, legs, and head are frozen stiff. He tells me that he will not hurt me and that he is sorry that he can't change his appearance to be more human, like some other aliens can do.

Again, he tells me that we must leave. The next thing that I know, I am on his ship. I am in the same room that I was in during the previous visit. I find myself sitting nude. Sitting in what seems to be the same chair that I sat in during my previous visit. The room is dark but the screen that showed all types of pictures of my brain brightens the room to a dawn color. The scanner is also present. Again, he leaves and later brings back the instruments he used on my head, and again he performs the same procedure as in the previous visit, stopping when he gets more than one beep and correcting the beep, to beep only one time. As he does this, he looks at the screen. After he has gone over every millimeter of my skull, he tells me the exam is finished.

I tell him that I want to thank him for what he has done because he has saved me many hours of painful therapy. I ask him if I can ask some questions,

"First, I don't know your name."

He answers, "Ored."

"Why did you perform this procedure?"

"To remove mental torture."

"How does it work?"

"I do not have time to explain it. It is secret and still in the testing stage, and besides, the human race has made such a mess of everything that they have invented that I would be afraid to let them know about this procedure."

"Has this equipment been used on other people?"

"No, it is experimental. There are still some things that need to be fixed."

"Like what?"

"Performing only one visit."

"Will future checkups be required?"

Ored said he didn't know. "We will have to evaluate all the results obtained in both visits."

"Will it be used on other people in the future?"

Ored said that he didn't know and that it was not up to him. "Who makes the decision?"

"The governing board or committee."

"What governing board?"

He said that he didn't have time to discuss the way his society is run and that he has little interest in that field.

I said, "This equipment would be a great gift for our doctors. So much good could be done."

"And so much harm if it fell into the wrong hands." His group of people could not live with themselves if that happened. "Maybe sometime in the distant future your race could use it right."

"Has your race used it as a weapon?"

"Definitely no."

At this point, Ored states he must leave and I must return.

At this time, I awaken.

Andrew's Fourth Essay: September 6, 1997

Today, I have to thank my therapist and the group I belong to. They were always there for me and helped me in many ways. I must also thank Ored. With his equipment, he was able to remove the trauma that seemed to cause my panic attacks, flash backs, and fears. Yes, I can still see the "grays" and I know I have been abducted. I also know that terrible things were done to me, but there are no feelings there. I have not had any recent visits from the grays.

Today, people tell me I look so much better. I feel better but I can't tell most people why. There may be a future problem. No, not with me, but with my wife. She told me that sometimes she wakes up to find one drop of blood on her bedding. The spot appears in different places. It's very hard to get just one drop of blood, especially since there is no wound.

Note from Constance:

In a subsequent group discussion, all of the experiencers in the room reported that they occasionally find one drop of blood on their sheets. In each instance, the drop of blood was described as being perfectly round and the size of a dime. The three "non-experiencers" in the room, including myself, could not recall ever having had such an experience.

The Shadow People

Date of Incident: October 17, 1997 Date of Session: October 22, 1997

Note from Constance:

Any hopes I had of Andrew's experiences being over were dispelled when he called in October to set up another appointment. I had wanted to complete the book with Andrew's story on a positive note.... so much for my plans!

Andrew reported that he had awakened Saturday morning with a headache. His leg was stinging and burning and when he examined it, he found two strange marks. One appeared to be a ring of small cuts forming an imperfect circle with a puncture mark in the center. He said that when he touched it, it hurt all the way to the bone. The second mark was a puncture wound surrounded by a partial circle of disconnected red marks.

He asked if I would bring a camera to our session and photograph his leg. It was four days before I could see Andrew and my point and shoot camera did not focus very well, but this is what his leg looked like.

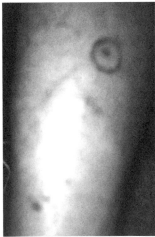

Figure 70

Andrew had no other clues to go on this time until under hypnosis, he recalled "a bit of a dream". The following are my notes from the session.

Andrew: I was sucked out of my shop like a flash. The flash stopped and I fell on the ground. I was picked up. I started to move again. I was dropped again.

Constance: Where are you?

Andrew: On the ground, in the grass. I'm wearing my blue jeans. I'm raised up again. I just lie there for awhile, but something is strange. I notice myself. There are two of me. I see myself lying above the ground. I'm solid, then I'm not solid. I'm close enough to see branches going through me.

Constance: What are you feeling?

Andrew: I'm scared. I don't like this.

Observation from Constance: A tear rolls down from Andrew's right eye.

Andrew: I don't have any control.

Observation from Constance: Tears roll down from Andrew's left eye.

171

Andrew: I feel like I'm in limbo, both of me. I don't have shoes on. I feel a pulling force. It seems like there's a malfunction or something. That's why they dropped me. There is no sound. I see the lights of the houses. I see the night light in the shop. Benji is in the house. I am being drawn to the creek behind my house. They've cleaned out that area. You can pretty well see at a distance. I can see cars going down the road a block away from me. I'm moving slowly. I went out of the door of the shop (not through the wall). I don't like this. I'm four to five feet above the ground. I'm not really solid. There are times when I am solid.

The ship is there. It's doing the same thing that I'm doing. It's solid one minute and not the next minute. I can see right through it. It's real funny. I haven't seen this craft before. It has a large oblong top, not like an egg. It's flatter and it widens out at the end. There must be six open squares, like a box with open ends. These objects that look like jet engines are going around the ship.

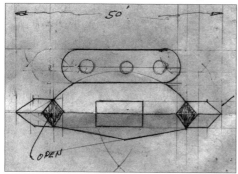
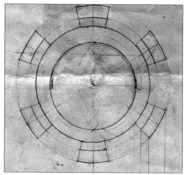

Figure 71   *Figure 72*

When car lights cross the bridge, the ship becomes transparent. I still see the outline of the ship. I don't want to go in.

Constance: How do you go in?

Andrew: Through the bottom, there's no hole, nothing to enter. I go in while the craft is in the transparent state. Oh no, I don't like this. I've never seen them before. They're 4'6" to 4'8" in height. I don't see any clothes. They appear as shadows. Some are black shadows with white eyes and some are white shadows with black eyes. Their heads are more oblong shaped, like a flat circle, or an ellipse. Their eyes stick out from their head. They have a bunch of small holes on each side of their head. They have one to three nostrils. The mouth is not on the

172

face, but underneath the face, under their chin. They fade in and out. There are six of them. Four white and two black.

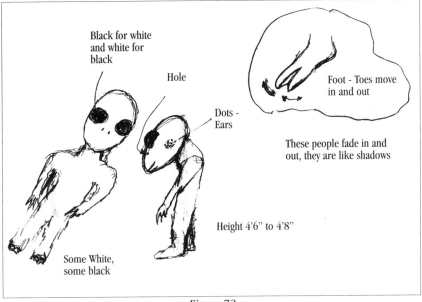

Figure 73

Constance: What are they doing?

Andrew: They're looking at me. My other self is there. It seems like they've made a duplicate of me. I appear to be going into shadow like they are. They don't say anything. There is no communication. One of them is taking a cord from the ceiling. He's attaching it to my leg with suction. It hurts like a knife cutting my leg. I don't like this. I tell them I'm hurting. They don't understand anything that I'm saying. It hurts all the way up to my stomach. My left leg is burning. The cord they are using seems to be flexible. It has a tube and in the end of the tube there's a needle. There's something glowing around the outside of the needle. It's not a constant thing. The color is sort of moving around and around. I think this causes the mark on my leg.

The black one attaches another cord. It's cold. There are two of me. Both have feelings.

Constance: Where are you?

Andrew: I'm on a table. Two black ones are working on my left leg. They fade out. Four white ones come in and start working on my leg. They fade away and the black ones come back in. One of them is drawing fluid now. The white one is going to remove the tube.

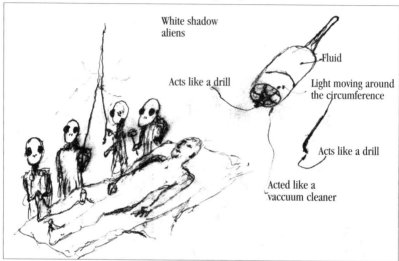

White shadow
aliens

Acts like a drill

Fluid

Light moving around
the circumference

Acts like a drill

Acted like a
vaccuum cleaner

Figure 74

Constance: How do you feel?

Andrew: Relief, like I've got my leg back again. I don't have my blue jeans on. I'm wearing nothing. They're going to remove me from the table. I'm going outside just like I came in. I can smell the creek. It stinks of stagnant sulfur water. They just dropped me there. I've got to walk home.

I remember my blue jeans lying beside me on the cement. I remember putting my blue jeans on. Yes, I do! I remember they did something to my ears. They used a big cotton swab. It made me feel sort of light-headed. There was no pain. It was a pleasant feeling.

Note from Constance:

After coming out of hypnosis, Andrew told me that he dreaded these beings worse than the others, as he felt he had no control. In all my work with him, this was only the second time he had cried while in trance. I could feel his helplessness. At least the other beings had maintained some telepathic communication with Andrew, allowing him to ask questions. But these beings, whom Andrew called "The

Shadow People", made no effort to communicate at all. When they were through with him, they dumped him by the creek, leaving him to find his way home in the dark.

At the end of our session, I suggested we place a call to Dr. Lerma, a wonderful physician we had recently found, through Maggie, whose story you will read next. Dr. Lerma is a pharmacologist and is board certified in internal medicine. He was in when I called and offered to see Andrew right away. I accompanied Andrew to his office and within a few minutes, Dr. Lerma had examined and x-rayed Andrew's leg. He also suggested a blood work-up and an MRI, as he was concerned about Andrew's recurrent headaches.

Dr. Lerma described the wound as a "circumferential biopsy-type lesion". He said, "The outer ring appeared to be formed by a suction apparatus and the biopsied area appeared to have been exposed to high temperatures, as seen with cautery or LASER burns." He said the wound did not look infected, but he gave Andrew antibiotics as prophylaxis. The x-rays of Andrew's leg were unremarkable.

Ten days later, Dr. Lerma examined Andrew's leg again. The follow-up on the skin revealed a "smooth hairless pinkish surface". He explained that in a controlled burn, such as that caused by a LASER, the skin may be void of hair follicles and heal similarly to Andrew's leg. He went on to say that Andrew's blood work had revealed a high lymphocyte count. Bone marrow and infectious causes were ruled out. Dr. Lerma said that high lymphocyte counts have been observed in astronauts and are associated with periods of weightlessness.

I think Dr. Lerma's quick and compassionate medical response meant a great deal to Andrew. At last, here was a physician group members could go to and tell the whole truth.

As for Andrew's anxiety symptoms, time will tell whether they will return. At least Ored's promise to keep the Grays away hadn't been broken, and Andrew seemed to take some solace in that. He said he hoped this would be a one time encounter with "The Shadow People".

175

Half 'n Half

Date of Incident: November 9, 1997 Date of Session: November 20, 1997

Note from Constance:

Less than three weeks later, on a chilly night when Benji refused to come inside the house, Andrew reported another strange occurrence. Not sure if it was a dream or an encounter, Andrew remembered waking up to go to the bathroom and seeing a half human, half alien being at the foot of his bed. He said he felt sexually aroused and found himself thinking he'd seen uglier women on Earth. Andrew drew a picture of his night apparition and arranged an appointment with me to find out if there was more to the experience than he consciously remembered. Here are my notes from that session, along with Andrew's picture.

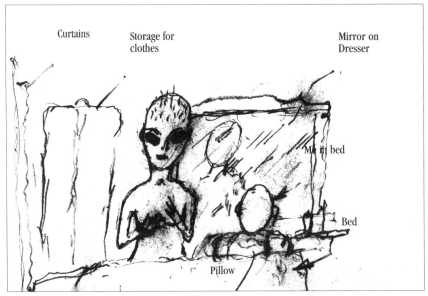

Figure 75

Andrew: I can see myself lying in bed and I sit up in bed. I wake and I sit up in bed and I guess I feel like I'm not awake, not fully awake. There seems to be a flash in the room. It doesn't last very long. It's like lightening lit up my room. During the next flash, this being is there and she's motioning me to come to her. I sit there awhile and notice the flashes as they occur. She's not one of them. She's half alien, half human. She's got a small mouth and nose, and extremely small

176

ears, smaller than the Grays. She's 4'10" to 4'11" in height. She has a thumb and 3 fingers with long, long, long, sharp fingernails. She's using both hands to motion me to come.

I'm telling myself "I don't really want to be a part of this." I'm afraid I'm either dreaming or it's a trick. Mentally, she talks with me. Evidently she understands that I don't want to go. "Come with me, I won't hurt you. Come with me," she says. "Why are you rejecting me?"

As I look at her, for her frame, she's very well-built, as far as shape goes. If I had to guess her age, I would guess her to be in her twenties. There's something that's real striking to me. There are no nipples on her breasts, and she has no navel. She has female sex organs, where the others didn't have any, yet the pubic hair is sparse. It's sprigged. I'm telling myself that I've seen uglier women on earth.

Constance: Does that surprise you?

Andrew: Yes, it's very surprising 'cause I don't expect to see a pleasant- looking alien. I'm wondering, what if this is a child of mine, taken from sperm many years ago? She seems to be in a cage, encased in something.

She doesn't understand why I don't come with her, she says "Please come with me." I'm telling myself "Keep your distance." Something inside is saying, "Don't be drawn into this. What if you're drawn in and you can't get back out? Have you thought about this, Andrew?" This reminds me of stories of the sirens who lure the sailors to their deaths.

I get up and she's more directly at the foot of my bed. I edge real close to my dresser, around the highboy, and I get out of the door. She's pleading with me, "But you really need to...". I'm telling myself, I just don't want to be a part of it. I go to the bathroom and when I come back, there's nothing there.

Note from Constance:

In talking about this experience, Andrew expressed feeling torn. He described it as fighting another mental battle. Though he felt sexually attracted to this being, he didn't trust her. He was troubled by the idea that she could be his daughter. If that was true, maybe he should have gone with her, but he said he was getting some signals warning him and somewhere in his mind, he felt like she was a decoy who came instead of the usual guy.

This was the first time Andrew had been able to move in the presence of a "visitor" and he had elected to leave the room. Toward the end of the session, Andrew burst into laughter as he recalled one of his favorite expressions from childhood: "My mother didn't raise any dumb children."

Though I don't know what the future holds for Andrew, I'm fairly certain that if I wait for his experiences to stop, I will never complete this book. Based on current results, I can say that Andrew's case is a therapeutic success. The change in him is readily apparent to all who know him. In spite of continuing encounters, Andrew no longer reports flashbacks, panic attacks, tremors, depression, or anxiety. Perhaps most importantly, he no longer doubts his own sanity.

Update from Constance: July 1998

In the nine months that have transpired since I wrote the above note, Andrew has continued to have periodic alien encounters. So far, the Grays have not returned, but the beings who have shown up in their place are worse. In spite of this, Andrew was holding up well emotionally until he recently encountered a being so intimidating that he was afraid to verbalize what he recalled under hypnosis. Apparently, this being threatened him with severe consequences if he told anyone what he'd seen.

Forced once again to keep a terrible secret, Andrew became acutely depressed. When I saw him a few weeks later, his hands were trembling and he was experiencing horrifying nightmares. He decided to tell me what he'd seen during our last session and he showed me the pictures he had drawn of the being and his ship. Again we attempted hypnosis and this time he was able to verbalize what he recalled. By the end of the session, his hands had stopped shaking. As he was leaving I told him I was glad he had decided to tell me what had happened. He laughed and said, What's the worst thing they could do to me, kill me and ruin my day?"

When the group met a week later, Andrew reported that his nightmares had continued and that he was having severe headaches. With some trepidation, he shared his latest experience with the group. Again, I noticed how much more relaxed he looked by the end of the meeting. Bottom line, no matter what else may be true, living with fear is a very destructive thing and having to keep secrets makes us sick.

Chapter Six

Never Ending Reality

Prologue to Maggie's Story

When the Friday Night Group began, we agreed on two ground rules. First, all discussions would remain confidential and second, the meetings would be closed except to people invited by present group members. Though we didn't state it as a rule, the group adopted the practice of informing the group ahead of time when they planned to bring a guest.

As the group was forming in the summer of 1996, Andrew was befriending a school counselor named, Maggie. She shared his interest in the subject of UFO's, and after several discussions she confided in him that she thought she was an experiencer. Andrew invited her to attend our group.

Due to her large expressive eyes and melodious voice, Maggie seemed younger than her forty-seven years. A divorced woman with three grown daughters and a grandchild, Maggie was working toward her second master's degree while holding down a full time job. The demands of her graduate studies, coupled with her teaching schedule, made it impossible for her to attend regularly, but the group took to her immediately. Two of Maggie's lovely daughters have also visited the group.

Although Maggie's story unfolded in a different culture, her ways of internalizing her anomalous experiences and her desperate efforts to cope with them, mirror those of the other women in this book. Unlike Kay and Lydia who underwent hypnosis before writing their stories, Maggie had only her conscious memories to draw on when she wrote her story.

Maggie's Account: Written November 1996

My name is Maggie. I come from the island of Puerto Rico, also known as the Island of Enchantment (Isla del encanto). Many strange things have happened in my life since I was a small child. These strange experiences made me feel different from the rest of the so called "normal" human beings. It was very difficult growing up with the feeling that I did not fit the norm that society demanded. My teenage years were no better. My self-esteem was very low. I also thought that I must be going crazy when these strange things occurred. I remember constantly praying because I had heard that crazy people had devils inside of them, so I was constantly praying to God to surround me with good angels that would protect me from evil. I was raised a Baptist, so the Bible was a big refuge for me. It was scary to speak to anyone about my experiences because they looked at me in a funny way, as if I was really crazy or retarded.

I had no one to turn to because I felt embarrassed to speak about the strange things that I saw that frightened me. But I really longed to have someone to speak to, especially during my teenage years. I guess that is why I prayed so much. The only one that I felt would listen with a loving smile and understanding was God and His Son, Jesus Christ.

My life has been quite lonely in that I needed to speak to someone about my experiences and there was no one to speak to and no one that would listen. Those that did listen would later reject me, like I was some kind of weird thing. So as I got older, I began to block a lot of things from my mind and even deny to myself that a lot of the experiences that I had gone through were true. I guess that is why now, at the age of 47, I recall very little.

It has been very difficult for me to consciously recall detailed descriptions of things beyond my human comprehension. Nevertheless, my conscious mind has allowed me to recall minute things, that years later I realized were actually part of my life. Well, I guess that I am not crazy after all. I am just one of those regular "normal" beings.

Though the majority of my recollection of extraordinary things are still vague and in my subconscious, I feel that I remember enough information to be able to share with others my personal experiences. I will, in the near future, find the time and the courage to go for some hypnosis sessions. I feel that the hypnosis sessions will help me tremendously. I have a positive feeling that they will help me in understanding a great part of my life that is now unknown. It is scary for me to unveil myself at this time.

Having been born and raised in Puerto Rico gave me a rich cultural upbringing, and background which included the island's superstitions. Believing in ghosts and supernatural deities has always been a part of our traditions. So ever since I was very small (2 or 3 years of age), whenever I saw something out of the ordinary, I would refer to it as a ghost. I recall being so scared that I would scream at the top of my lungs, until someone came to rescue me from whatever I had seen.

I recall having a happy childhood while growing up. I was the baby in a house full of adult females, so all of the attention was placed on me. My mom was 19 years old when I was born. During the Great Depression, she was forced to go to Florida and work, in order to send my grandmother money to care for me, and feed us all. She was a single mom. My dad had left with someone else while she was pregnant. Times were very rough then, but I had lots of moms to care for me, and plenty of love and attention. So my childhood days overall, were very happy ones.

I can consciously recall something strange happening to me at around age 2 or 3. I was walking some yards ahead of my youngest aunt, who was around 18 years of age at the time, and my grandmother, when I saw something, or felt something that I cannot recall, and fainted. Both my aunt and my grandmother ran to see what had happened, but they couldn't understand the cause. Minutes later I was back to myself, and the incident was forgotten. Years later when it was brought up in a casual conversation by my aunt, she still could not understand what had come over me, nor could I remember the details.

My grandmother, bless her heart, died when I was around 4 years of age. My mom had married while in Florida, so after my grandmother died, I went to Florida to live with her, my step-dad and my younger sister. Later on, my mom gave birth to my brother. It was tough for me to adjust to the new life style and language, but step by step I did it. I did long for the attention that I was used to.

We lived in Miami, Florida. My step-dad had been learning to weld, and worked in this field until he decided that he could manage his own business. In the meantime, we lived in a nice little house next to a field where nature surrounded our back yard. I loved going out into our back yard and disappearing into the vast jungles of pine trees and bushes, where on many an occasion I would have to run back to my house because wild mother birds would be pecking at my head for having peeked into their nests or touched one of their young. In that nice little house, I also remember huge black snakes bathing in the sun right in front of our front porch. It was exciting for me. For some reason, I just loved the nature around me. It was there too that strange things began to emerge.

I began to see someone or something in the bedroom where we slept. I was around 6 or 7, already in elementary school. My screams would penetrate the neighborhood. I was terrified. My poor mom was also terrified because she did not know what it was that I was seeing. I remember my step-dad checking outside of our home, since we lived in such an open area, though we had neighbors to the left of us.

This situation went on for several years. I would say it was a ghost. I had no other way of describing what it was that I was looking at. I remember once describing the form of a man, and saying that he was smoking because I remembered seeing smoke, but I'm not sure now, if my description was correct,. Because of our island superstitions, my mom would bring different people into the house to relieve it of evil spirits and would also have the church ministers and priests come to pray for all of us and request God to cast out evil spirits. I dreaded seeing the sun set, that meant having to face night. I would cover my body completely under the blankets, including my head. I did not want to see anything and it took me forever to go to sleep. I got jumpy, my nerves were always on end, especially at night. I wasn't getting the rest I needed at that age because of these strange happenings. Later we moved.

This second house was more closely surrounded by other houses. The yard was huge. I do not recall this second house that well, probably because we did not live in it as long. Nevertheless, strange things did happen. I remember once at age 9, during Christmas time, looking out of my bedroom window and seeing Santa Claus and his reindeer passing across the sky. I was all excited and told my parents, unfortunately in front of company, that I had just seen Santa Claus with his reindeer flying across the sky. I received a very stern face from my mom who told me that I must have been dreaming (she was very embarrassed), my step-dad told me to go to bed and the company visiting our house was just laughing at what I had said. I felt really humiliated, especially since I had been staring out of the window and knew for sure what I had seen.

For some reason, I have always been fascinated with our universe, our constellations and everything that has to do with celestial bodies. I have had a deep loving feeling for nature. I have always felt very close to the trees and flowers, as if I could embrace them with my heart and they could return my embrace in their own particular way. I have always felt this, ever since I was a young child. I have felt very connected to nature.

Then we moved again. This time into a home that would give me a real taste of horror. A dreaded horror that changed my good nature into rebellion against my parents. My own parents were wondering if I was mentally sick in some way. They could not understand the frustration, terror and all the mixed up feelings that I had because of feeling I was different, without wanting to. Family members also commented on how sad it was that I was such a mentally retarded person (their concept of mental retardation). My school grades went down, my parents would always tell me that I would have to go work in a shrimp factory because that was the only thing that I was good for. My self-esteem was very low. I started having problems with teachers and school. I began playing hooky, and mixing with the wrong crowd, but still my problems were not solved and I had no escape. The only thing that kept me going even when I knew that I was doing things the wrong way, was my praying to God. I would ask Him to help me and protect me and to help me understand what was happening to me.

My step-dad had his own business by now, so we lived in a pretty good area and had all the commodities needed. I shared a room with my sister. The rooms were pretty spacious. I remember that we had twin beds and that we had our beds located on opposite walls. We had a big chest of drawers to one side of the room and a large vanity chest of drawers towards the foot of our twin beds, centralized. From the foot of our twin beds to the vanity chest there was plenty of room left where my mom had placed a nice carpet. The floor was all tile. The room had two screened windows, with outside glass that was opened by an inside handle. In this house I spent the rest of my childhood days up until I was 16 years old.

Moving into this house looked bright at the beginning, but then things started to happen. I would hear knocks on the cement wall where my bed was located. There would be around three knocks, silence and again the knocks would start. I would respond by knocking back with the same amount of knocks. This seemed like a game to me and I never thought about negative consequences. I

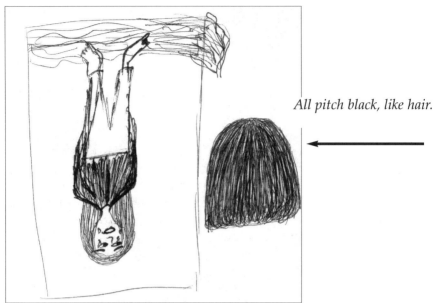

All pitch black, like hair.

Figure 76

cannot recall how long this knocking game took place up until I began to be uncovered at night and wake up with a big black bulk of what seemed like hair next to me. This experience topped all of what I had seen. I was terrified of that black thing, whatever it was. It would not move, it never made a sound, it was just there. I would try to scream but nothing seemed to come out. I felt nobody could hear me or help me. I was afraid to tell my parents, so I kept it to myself as I recall. People laughed at what I told them that I had experienced, so I felt that I couldn't trust anyone. I used to hide and cry because of my frustration and even began to have doubts about myself.

During one particular night in that same house, I remember that my sister had heard the same knocking as I had. I was amazed because for some reason she was scared of it. I became brave and told her that there was nothing that she had to be afraid of and showed her by knocking on the wall that it was nothing. During that night I could not sleep. My sister was sound asleep but I was tense, afraid, wanting to jump in bed with my mom, but knowing that it would be an embarrassment for a 13 or 14-year-old to do this. Finally I fell asleep but awoke to find that I was uncovered and the black thing was at my bed side. I remember screaming but no sound coming out. I began to pray, and then I fell asleep, to wake up in the morning very tired.

Other things that I remember seeing were images. Images of people, that were very transparent. These I have seen ever since I was very small. My mother would say that these were angels or that these were relatives that were with me to protect me. These were the words that calmed me down when I was a little girl, getting older and going to church made me realize that entities were not necessarily something good. I was very scared of seeing things out of the ordinary and this went on in this last house that my step-dad had bought. Then my step-dad's father died in Puerto Rico. Miami was becoming violent because of racial problems between whites and blacks, and Castro had overpowered Cuba and loads of refugees were streaming into Florida. All of these circumstances made my father decide to go back to our enchanted island.

Moving was great. It felt like a new beginning and in a way it was. I did not know my Spanish, so I had to learn it. I had just turned 16 when we returned to Puerto Rico. I felt relief. This was an escape for me from so many strange things. Surely, whatever it was wouldn't cross the ocean, every strange and horrifying thing would stay in Florida. New friends also meant that they knew nothing about me and I definitely would not say anything to anyone to mess up the friendship. My self-esteem started to rise. I felt I had a chance.

Once we got settled in the rented house that we moved into, I started to see the black figure of a person. The unusual thing not only occurred during the night but also during the day. I would be washing dishes and I would see a dark figure of a man, wearing something similar to a frock used by monks, but it was like black cloth with a hood. I would run out of the kitchen or room where I was located and start to scream that I had seen a ghost. I even had visions that seemed like huge T.V. screens in front of me, that would appear and just as fast disappear. During one of these visions, I had seen our parakeet cage fall and our parakeets fly out, then the vision was gone. I wondered what it meant and why I had witnessed that vision. During the late afternoon of that same day, I was going to see if our parakeets were okay and bring them into the house. When I lifted up the cage, the bottom of the cage came loose and the parakeets started to flutter. I was quick enough to bring the cage down in order to catch one of the parakeets that was ready to fly off. One flew away. This incident had me wondering why it happened and why I got a vision of it hours before.

185

I continued to experience ghosts even after we moved into a house that my father had bought, along with a big piece of land. Here I felt intimidated by the entities. Many nights, I woke up feeling paralyzed, wanting to scream, but being unable to. My sister and I shared a big bed together and at times I woke up because of something hitting me across the face. It felt like a folded up towel. It was scary, especially when I would be brave enough to look around the room and not see anything or anyone. I was definitely stronger than ever on praying and had a lot of faith in God. He was the only one to know why this was happening and I just had to wait until I had the permission of understanding it all.

During one night, I was already in the university studying. I was the only one up. I felt something deep inside my stomach, like I knew something strange would be happening to me that night. I started to pray. I was situated in the center of the house where the dining room was located. In back of me was the kitchen and beyond that was my brother's room that led to the back yard. In front of me was the living room and in front of that was the porch. On the right side of me were my sister's and my bedroom and in front of our room was my parent's room. I continued feeling very uneasy and strange until I felt I was being looked at from behind. I was so scared. I did not want to look back because I was not ready to see what I dreaded. I continued to pray and ask God to help me cope with whatever evil was around me. I knew that my brother was sleeping in the bed and I knew that it was not him. I knew for sure that it was not human. Then I felt relief as I sensed that whatever was there was going away. All of a sudden I heard the chickens all upset, dogs began to bark, and I knew that whatever was there had gone back out of our home. My brother never felt anything. I was fully awake during this experience. I took off into my room, jumped into bed and covered myself. I don't even remember if I turned off the light to the room, probably not.

A few years later I married and still the strange things continued. Not as scary as when I was a little girl. I guess I outgrew the fear or something. I do get scared, but not as scared as before. My daughters have also experienced things that are not human. It runs in my family, I guess. My life has truly been a never-ending reality reach, as far as strange things go.

A never-ending reality that took its aim at the children that I bore after I married. I had my first child at age twenty-four. During my pregnancy, something happened that made me aware of being careful. From that time on, I've locked my apartment door, and re-checked locks on doors and windows before retiring to bed. I was very scared to tell my husband of the incident because I did not want to upset him, and because it was a very delicate and embarrassing situation. The incident occurred as follows:

During my first pregnancy, because of the tropical heat, I was accustomed to sleeping topless and uncovered. I would place a mosquito net around the bed and tuck it beneath the mattress, before turning out the lights, and falling asleep. However, one strange night when I was seven or eight months into the pregnancy, while my husband and I were asleep, something woke me up. I didn't know why, but I was very frightened.

I remember awakening with fear, and opening my eyes just a little, to see what was going on in the room. I wanted to wake up my husband who was sleeping next to me, but I was afraid to, and he was very sound sleeper. As I looked around the room, and into part of the kitchen area, I saw a man, or I think it was a man. I couldn't see his features because of the darkness, but I saw his figure. I was very frightened then, I felt sure that if I screamed, or even moved, he might try to kill both my husband and me. I remember staying very still, and trying to see what the person was doing. Then he started walking softly into our bedroom. I felt terrified, cold, paralyzed. I began to pray silently that this person would just go away. Then something horrifying happened. The person stuck his arm through our mosquito net, then cupped my left breast. As he did this, I felt a flash of electricity run through my entire body.

Next thing I knew, it was morning. I still felt scared, but the morning light gave me courage to check the apartment. I was so scared that I don't remember checking to see if our doors and windows were tampered with, or open. One thing is for sure, I was happy that we were still alive. I never told my husband. I was very embarrassed about the whole thing, and after that I never slept topless again. I also left the lights on at night to go to sleep, something that I still do to this day.

The child I was carrying, has suffered from petite mal seizures, from the time she was in elementary school until now, although she has gotten better. There have also been problems when she is working on a computer, or other electrical equipment or devices. They tend to mess up easily, even when she is just walking in front of a computer, it messes up. I have often wondered if it has anything to do with those things I experienced before she was born.

My second child has had out-of-body experiences and my third (last child) has seen things, and has suffered from recurring nose bleeds, which started during her pre-adolescent years. All of these things are so overwhelming at times. The saddest thing is that you are not in control. It (whatever it is) dominates, controls, takes without asking, and makes a mess of its victims (fear, especially).

Hopefully, one day what is happening will come out into the open, in order for qualified professional people to help victims like my offsprings and myself cope with the problems. What is happening is very real.

Note from Constance:

Eight months after Maggie wrote her story, I called her to see how she was doing. She said she was recovering from surgery and she told me with excitement what had happened to her the first time she saw her new physician, John Lerma. Determined to take advantage of her summer break, Maggie was trying to finish reading Whitley Strieber's book, *Communion*. She had taken it with her to read while she was waiting for the doctor. She had removed the cover of the hardback book so that no one would see what she was reading. When the nurse led her into Dr. Lerma's office, Maggie set her purse on top of the book and sat on the examining table across the room. The doctor entered the room, sat down facing her and immediately turned his head 180 degrees and bending his head over to the side, he read the title from the spine of her book. Maggie said he then looked at her and asked, "Do you believe in aliens?" When she answered that she wasn't sure, he asked, "Are you having experiences?" Maggie told him that "since he put it that way," that she thought she was. He proceeded to spend the next hour and a half listening to her and when his nurse complained that he had patients waiting, he told her he was "with a patient."

I later learned that Dr. Lerma had been praying that patients who were having abduction experiences would find their way to him, as he felt drawn to help them. This was incredible, since the group had expressed the need for a physician who could deal with the medical after-effects of their abduction experiences. I had called Whitley Strieber months earlier to see if he knew of a physician in our area who was open to treating abductees, but at the time he didn't. Not knowing how else to search, I had just been waiting for a response from the universe and thanks to Maggie, here it was.

When the group met the following week, I shared Maggie's exciting news and they requested that I invite Dr. Lerma to our next meeting. By the time I called him, I had heard stories from two other people about his exceptional diagnostic abilities. He agreed to attend and when I learned that he wanted to meet Whitley Strieber, I invited Whitley and his wife Anne to attend as well. Since then, Dr. Lerma has become an invaluable resource to the members of the group and has worked with Whitley on his implant research.

As for Maggie, she attends the meetings when she can and she tells me that being a part of the group has made her feel much better about herself.

Chapter Seven

One Small Step for Humankind

Prologue to Sara's Story

Our last story comes from Daniel's wife, Sara, who, as a special education teacher, ranks among the saints in my book. I don't know what it is about Sara, but one feels warmth and acceptance in her presence. Always patient with Daniel's mischievous streak, Sara seems to have a grounding effect on him and because she listens so well, she has also become indispensable to the group.

Sara has faithfully attended "the therapy group", as she calls it, since its inception. To date, she has chosen not to undergo hypnosis, maintaining that what she consciously remembers is scary enough.

The irony is that of all the members of the group, Sara was the one who started having lucid experiences, experiences she could consciously remember upon awakening. She did this the hard way, by forcing herself to open her eyes and look at what was frightening her.

I discovered another bit of irony in Sara's story when I learned that she had been in therapy for treatment of her anxiety disorder two years earlier, and that the therapist she had seen was none other than my husband. During her sessions with him she had not confided what she suspected was the cause of her anxiety. Since my husband and I have different last names, Sara didn't realize the connection until she and Daniel arrived for his first appointment at The Harbor, the eighty year old, New England style house where my husband and I practice.

Sara's initial symptoms included anxiety, claustrophobia, fear of fog, and fear of the dark. She explained that she was unable to sleep if the closet door was open. Sara said she felt that she had no say in what happened to her and that in order to deal with her feelings she was driven to meditate. Interestingly enough, all that was about to change as Sara was about to break through her amnesia and master her fear.

Introduction By Daniel:

Sara's family lived in the back country of New Mexico for a number of years. Strange sounds, cattle mutilations, odd sightings and other instances of the UFO phenomenon were quite common in the area and it didn't take long before her family joined the surrounding ranchers in seeing their share of strange things in the skies. The people who live in that area don't make much of what they've seen and are typically unwilling to speak of what they've seen to outsiders. It's both because they don't want to be troubled with the curious or skeptical and because they themselves aren't terribly interested. Their lives are a far more serious struggle for economic survival than most of us might imagine and there's little time for the red light Mr. Davis saw over his barn the other night. Like whistling past a graveyard, often the feeling is that the less said, the better.

Odd beeping noises, roaring noises like that of huge jet engines overhead, strange blue lights in their bedrooms, even vehicle sightings in the night, and occasionally daytime, skies were all taken in stride and soon became part of the web of inside family jokes and stories—to be discussed only with other family members if at all— and mostly ignored.

Sara, her sisters, and her mother all developed similar psychological problems; including anxiety attacks, claustrophobia, depression, fear of the dark, and sleeplessness. They fought these problems on their own, accepting them as a normal part of the stresses of modern life. Not until later did they begin to connect these problems with the pattern of abductions that began to emerge.

I was reading Budd Hopkin's *Missing Time* and Sara had the opportunity to read Whitley Strieber's *Communion*. The face on Strieber's cover jacket triggered a strong fear response in Sara when she saw it. She had to remove the jacket before she could read further. At about that time, her parents hooked up with a group of UFO researchers in Albuquerque, one of whom began to relate his experiences. One evening, over dinner, Sara asked her mother if she remembered seeing the UFO on the dirt road leading to their old ranch and the flood gates were opened. One memory led to another and they were soon forced to realize that all those strange events were even stranger than they had imagined. All of them were apparently abductees of considerable experience.

This has been a terrifying journey, but Sara cannot emphasize enough the importance of a strong family in coping with the experiences. "The rest of the world thinks we're crazy and without the internal strength of our family, we might have become convinced we are crazy," she explains. Sara says her younger sister still has not faced the reality of what has been happening and the stress is showing in all aspects of her life. Sara's father endures intense headaches and bouts of almost unmanageable fear whenever the topic lingers around the dinner table over long.

Aside from me, whose curiosity won't permit me to ignore this, none of Sara's family has undergone hypnosis. That may come, but for the moment, what they remember consciously is already sufficiently frightening. However, all of us are convinced that we will soon know, without doubt, the true nature of these events. There is a sense of expectancy surrounding our lives that is intriguing at best, terrifying at worst. The answers are pending.

Sara's Account: Written December 1996

My first conscious memory of being abducted was many years ago, in New Mexico while I was home on spring break from college. We had gone into town and were on the way home. My sister Kate and I had made this deal that when we rode in the truck, I would sit next to the window on the way into town and she would sit next to the window on the way back. So, she was sitting next to the window on the passenger side and I was sitting in the middle. My mother was, of course, driving. It was a beautiful day, cool and clear, and I was feeling very happy. We were about six miles from the main highway, on the twenty-three mile dirt road that led to our ranch. I was looking over toward my mother's side of the pickup when I saw a huge, black object in the sky. It was long, big, and black. It reminded me of the X-15. There were some things sticking out of it, but I don't remember many details. I said to my mother, "Look at that! I wonder what that is?" "What is the government up to now?" she replied in a resigned, half-joking tone. I looked over to my right, and nothing was there. We continued to our home, but nothing more was ever said about our encounter. Not that day after we got home, or for fifteen years, was anything said about it.

The first therapist I saw suggested that I learn to meditate as a way to lower my anxiety. When I started learning to meditate, learning to make my mind blank, I began to remember other details about that day. By the time we met Constance, I had remembered the following details.

The truck stopped running, just stopped. "What is going on?" I asked. "I don't know," my mother said. I can hear the fear in her voice. I was very scared. My heart was pounding. My little sister was very upset and crying. She was still in elementary school at the time. Mother tried to calm her.

Suddenly I felt unable to move, not quite paralyzed, but unable to move. I was very upset, worried for my sister and could see that my mother felt terribly helpless. I saw three tall Grays approaching the truck, dressed in uniforms, approaching from the driver's side. The uniforms were silver in color, like silver cloth but not like aluminum foil. I think there was a belt. I don't remember seeing any other emblems or details.

Without transition, I'm in a room, very white, very sterile, with three tall Grays in the room with me. These were different; they weren't wearing the uniforms. They were naked, as far as I could tell. There's nothing else in the room. It's not very big, with a curved wall on one side, straight walls otherwise. I wanted to get back to my mother and my sister. I was very anxious, almost to the point of being sick, on the verge of throwing up. They reassured me that everything was all right. They didn't speak, the message was more of a feeling. They seemed very curious about why I was so upset about being away from my mother. I was very upset about being separated. They kept asking me questions about why I was upset. I told them that I love my mother, that we're close, and that I wanted to get back to my family and off this ship. I was remembering the time when I was a little girl going to have my tonsils out, being rolled out of the room on the gurney, watching my mother being left behind and screaming my head off.

That's all I can remember about this incident. I've avoided meditation since, not wishing to find out more, or maybe I'm afraid to find out more. My mother has since remembered some of the details about her experience, but it wouldn't be fair of me to report those here.

In another incident, here in our current house, I woke up with three small Grays standing next to my bed, on the side. My husband

and I sleep in separate bedrooms. I became very anxious, especially looking at their huge, black, almond-shaped eyes. They indicate to me that they want me to go with them. I told them "No!" and covered my face with the covers. Whether I went with them or not, I cannot say.

During Thanksgiving vacation at my parents house, since we've begun having the therapy groups, there was another incident. That evening, prior to going to bed, I had the feeling that the Grays were coming and I was nervous all night long. I was asleep on my stomach in the guest bedroom. I felt a long finger touch the side of my neck with a gentle touch. The finger felt soft, long and not solid like ours would feel. The touch was cold. There is a numbing sensation from the top of my head to the tips of my toes. It felt very familiar. I kept my eyes closed because I didn't want to see them. I tried to remain calm, but I knew what was happening. Then I'm lying on my stomach, my head drooping off the edge of a metal table. There were three Grays there, one on each side, one at my head. I felt their presence more than saw them. I felt one running its fingers through my hair, like they were looking for lice or something. There was a painful prick on the back of my neck. The aliens tried to comfort me. There was another prick, more painful this time, but I stayed still. There was yet another, still more painful prick. This time I yelled out and lifted my head against the pain. I opened my eyes and I could see the Gray's bodies but I couldn't see their faces. The one on my right side used his three fingers to press my head back down very gently. I will never forget the sensation of their touch. It is beyond description, but unforgettable.

Then I was lying in my bed, wondering what happened, feeling a little odd, but concluding I'd had a bad dream and just went back to sleep. I got up the next morning and was in the bathroom when I began remembering pieces of the incident. I'd just been discussing with Daniel his fears of my being abducted and not returned, so I chose not to discuss the incident with him right away. I described it later to Daniel on our return home. I wish now I'd said something so that we could have looked at my neck to see if there was a mark.

Note from Constance:

Soon after completing the above narrative, Sara had another encounter. Upon awakening the next morning, she tape recorded her memories of the experience. Daniel transcribed the tape exactly as she spoke it, editing only to remove noise and repair some grammatical awkwardness.

Sara's First Recording

Last night they came and they got me. I heard a funny noise and then I could feel myself getting numb all over. This numbing was really bothering my neck. I felt like I wanted to put my hand on my neck just to make myself feel better because I was getting scared. I was surprised that I was able to move my hand. I was thinking to myself, "Okay, this is going to make me feel better; my hand's here. This feeling in my neck is going to stop."

I'm lying on my side when this is happening. It's my left arm that I've moved. I feel these long fingers moving my hand, my arm, back down. This time, for some reason, they carry me out—because I can feel all these hands underneath me, carrying me out.

I kept my eyes shut. It seems like I always keep my eyes shut when it comes to this process. I'm in this room and I'm sitting on a table. I feel like I'm in my bedroom but I know I'm not. I feel like I'm sitting on my bed, but I know I'm not. I'm really agitated. I see two Grays standing in front of me and I'm waiving my arms around asking them why they're bugging this man who's in our group. "Why are you torturing him, why are you...why are you, why are these things happening? I mean he is just suffering so."

The two Grays sort of float out of the room and this alien comes in. Of course, he looks, I mean, to me, he looks like a human, but I know he's not. He's different from anyone that I have ever seen before. I mean, when I go, I see my regulars, or I see the same ones over and over, but this one is different.

They want to answer my questions. What they said was that, for some reason, some humans will not have their memory erased enough to prevent them from getting anxious. I don't know why I felt like he was a 'he', and of course he's not talking, I'm getting all this telepathically. He's saying, "Your mother has the same problem, you have the same problem, your sister has this same problem of being afraid." He said, "You humans have, and he referred to us a 'humans', have this fear reaction that's very, very strong". He said, "That's why we immobilize you, because we're afraid that you'll hurt us, because you have this fear reaction."

He said, and I thought this was really strange, "That's why we're always telling you to keep your eyes shut." I've always thought it was my idea, but it's really their idea that they're putting into my head.

Because they know that when they show up, it really startles me, so they encourage me to keep my eyes shut until I get where I'm going. Then I open my eyes.

He said that the whole problem is that some people just can't get their memories erased, or it doesn't work on them. I got really aggravated. I said, "But yeah, ok, so this is not working on him, but you still keep picking him up and still keep scaring him half to death."

I was really surprised because normally they don't say very much but he was really wanting me to understand. For some reason, he couldn't finish his conversation because something was happening to someone else that they were experimenting with that was not going right and he had to leave. I got the impression that the aliens have abductees that they train to be calmers. I think the reason this guy seemed human, and looked alright to me, was because he was another abductee that they have trained to be a calmer, and they sent him to talk to me.

He was a male. He had blonde hair. He was about five foot seven. He was medium built, and I could've sworn I'd seen this person before. But he was another abductee talking to me, trying to explain why this guy in our group was being pestered. He also mentioned the fact that he knew that they knew that we were meeting as a group. They feel that one of the big things that we have to try to get over is our fear, because he says, "As you get over your fear of us, you will get over your other fears." It's the fear that hurts us. It's the fear that makes whatever they do to us worse.

I know for Daniel, when he talks about it he knows it hurts, he knows something is going to happen, but he has gotten over this fear. I've gotten over, well, it's getting better, even though they tell me to keep my eyes closed.

It wasn't an alien, that I was seeing as a human, it was another abductee talking to me trying to explain, because I was really agitated. They didn't do anything as far as experiments, because they were concerned that I wanted to get this question answered.

Then he had to go, because they were having a problem with another abductee and he had to go. He said, "I'm sorry, but I have to go. I can't finish this conversation and I think they're gonna take you back now." I guess they did, because I woke up. Then, as I was eating breakfast, I began to remember. I made myself, like I did the last time when I was in my parents room, remember the sensation and remember what happened. This is the first time I have ever remembered, real clearly, what went on.

I said that the alien probably looked like a human to me in my eye, but what I think it is, it was not an alien, it was another abductee. In this book that I read, they talk about training abductees and I think this was just another abductee that has been trained to be a calmer.

The conversation I had with him is just fleeting, like a hundred miles an hour, through my mind. I'm trying to remember all this because I know if I don't talk about it now, it's going to be erased.

I remember now that I got the impression that he had blonde hair; he was five foot seven of medium build. I got the impression he was in the medical field because he was very calming. I was very surprised while I was asking these questions, he knew about this man, he knew about my mother, he knew about me, he knew about my sister and about our being anxious. I said I had to get back to Daniel and he said, "Oh, you will. They always send you back. They never keep anybody."

They said they had taken Daniel too and I was going to try to ask if they'd ever taken us together, and he couldn't, because he had to go to this other situation. I got the impression that another abductee was coming unglued and he had to go to calm him.

But I don't know whether they abducted me for me to talk to this guy, or what. But they didn't do anything to me and he was really going into, in the conversation, how they know how we react to fear. We become so scared and startle so easily and they are aware of it. I got the impression that what makes things worse when we're there is just our being afraid of it, because it is so different, and they are so different. They really don't want us to be scared, but we are.

I always used to think it was my idea to keep my eyes closed, but from the conversation, it is they that make that suggestion to close our eyes and that's why, a lot of times, they make us, say, go to sleep. It's like their way of knocking us out. They give us these suggestions so we won't become so startled. He went on to explain in detail about how that's why they erase the memories, because they know it'll drive us crazy. He said many people have this problem of being anxious and developing anxiety problems due to becoming a "chosen one" as he put it. I remember asking why, as a child, when they... We went into that, he said some of us are not picked up as children. He said there are just some that are not, but he said, many of us, the chosen ones, are picked as children and we're abducted all our lives. When we're children, we don't seem to be as afraid of them as when we become adults. Maybe Constance can explain why as adults we become so wrapped up and involved and we become anxious because of our fears. I don't ever remember becoming anxious as a child, but I do remember becoming a very anxious person as I became an adult.

What happens is we start remembering that we're being abducted and they try to eradicate it from our minds so we don't go crazy. But a lot of us do go crazy over this. I never got the impression whether they're sorry about it or not from this abductee but he did explain that's why they immobilize us. There are some that learn to get over it, and they allow us to go on, on our own.

This is the other really important thing I just remembered. Saturday, I really did a lot of housework and my feet were swollen and were bothering me. While I was on the ship, I felt absolutely no pain.

I realize now that the aliens speak to me telepathically, but he was not, he was speaking to me with his mouth. I don't remember exactly what he was wearing. I think he had on a white t-shirt and boxer shorts. He was in his late twenties, early thirties.

< End recording >

Note from Sara:

Shortly after this incident, we had one of our regular group meetings. Theresa was especially interested in my description of the young man who spoke with me. Through her questioning, I suddenly remembered he had the strangest deep blue eyes, penetrating, not of this earth. I've now begun to question my initial conclusion that he was human.

The therapy group has been vital to my well-being during these past months. We've grown rather like a family and I'm eternally grateful for the support they've given us.

Note from Constance:

I will never forget how animated Sara became following this lucid experience. Having long since reconciled herself to her own abductions, she was finally able to experience and express righteous indignation toward her captors, not for what they had done to her, but for what they had done to Andrew. She seemed vitalized as a result, and she felt good about overcoming her fears enough to remain aware.

Sara had another lucid experience on the morning of February 9, 1997 which she recorded upon awakening. Here is her account as transcribed by Daniel.

Sara's Second Recording

After Daniel fixed the thermostat, I went back to bed. I couldn't go to sleep, so I went out to the living room and sat in the rocking chair. I often go sit in the rocking chair when I can't sleep. It was probably around three o'clock or so. Someone touched me and I suddenly had the feeling of not being able to move. I started to fight it. I wanted to move, but then I said to myself, "Don't fight this." I remembered being told during my last abduction that if I get over the fear of them, I'll get over my other fears.

I said to myself, "Well, I'm going to try to open my eyes and see what's gonna happen." All the other times, I kept my eyes tightly shut. I opened my eyes and there stood a tall Gray. I was looking at him, not getting anxious, and I smiled a little to myself. He probably thought I was nuts. I noticed the room was illuminated with a bluish, white light. It lit up the whole room. There wasn't a specific beam and there were no shadows. I was a little scared but I got this feeling from him not to be scared. I started to grin again, you know, like "Oh, here we go again." I felt myself being pulled up, my whole body, it was like somebody was pulling at my chest, to pull me out of the chair. I didn't like that sensation.

Talking to myself, for the comfort of it, I thought "Oh, I don't like this!" I realized I was being pulled up! "Oh my God, I'm gonna be pulled through my house!" So I shut my eyes. I felt like I was floating. It was a really odd sensation, I really didn't like it. I wanted to open my eyes. I wanted to see where I was going, but I had this feeling that if I did, I might get sick because I don't like heights. It was a little like being car sick, dizzy and nauseated at the same time.

Then I'm standing in a room with other people. I didn't recognize anybody. The same Gray that came and got me was there. He told me that I'm to go into another room. It was not a very big room, the same, white, sterile, clean room I remember from before. There was another person on the table right next to me.

I remember I'm sitting on this table, metal, aluminum, silver-like. It reminded me of a veterinarian's table. A Gray is behind me. I can see his hands. I'm reminded of the hands that Lydia had drawn that we'd seen in the therapy group. I'm really looking at them, but the Gray becomes aware that I'm really studying his hands. He didn't make me stop, but he was aware of my study. Suddenly, he's running his hands through my hair, like he's looking for nits or something. The hands are cold. They're not warm. They feel long, and they feel very light.

I notice there's this person across from me. I don't recognize this person but it was a man and he looked absolutely terrified. I got the impression maybe this was his first time on the ship or he hadn't been on there very many times. He was terrified. I wasn't talking to him, but I was sending him this thought, "Just relax and sit still and it'll all be over with very soon. Don't, whatever you do, don't fight this, just try to relax and it'll all be over with."

I sent a telepathic thought! Then I thought to myself, I'm asking the Gray, did I think what I just did, I mean did I send this...and I got the impression of an answer, "Yes, I sent a telepathic thought." I said "I want to know how to do this all the time." "You can do it, but you people don't know how." This isn't a quote, more the gist of my understanding. Evidently I had this ability to do it on the ship.

And then I'm back in the first room again, with all these people. I'm getting really impatient. Whatever they do is over and I was anxious to go back home.

I see this young boy. He didn't seem anxious or afraid, just waiting like the rest of us. He was about eight or nine, with brownish hair. I was quite impressed with his calm demeanor. We were not supposed to be talking to each other. I wish they'd hurry up because I want to get back to Daniel.

I now remember seeing stars, and then a bright, bright light. So I must have had my eyes open for at least part of it. And then I'm in bed.

I remember waking up, but this time, when I woke up I was not sitting in the chair; they put me back on my bed. I don't know why they did that, but I guess they must have known I was having trouble sleeping and they wanted to put me back on my bed so I would sleep.

I just remembered that I commented to Daniel that feeling of being pulled out of my chair and remembering what Andrew said about feeling... Well, the whole time I was up there this time, I was trying to remember, and think of things that we were all discussing and yes, that smell, that smell, is definitely there. To me, it smells like mildew. That time I was up there, that's what it smelled like. I notice my nose is a little stuffed up today.

Sara's Letter to Constance: June 5, 1997

I remember this through a dream which has been bothering me for weeks. I wanted to bring it up during the last group, but I was embarrassed about it. Everything I'm about to describe, I remember fairly clearly.

I'm being put on a table by two tall Grays. I'm naked. I don't remember anything about the room—in my mind, it's dark and there's a light over the table. I feel like they don't want to hurt me, they're trying to be a gentle as possible. There's a tall Gray on either side of me. The one on my right gently spreads my legs apart. I do not resist. I do not feel very happy about this, but there's no real resistance in me. They have this small, dumbbell-shaped object that they insert into my vagina. It goes in rather smoothly and does not hurt. They leave it in there a few minutes and then just take it out. I have the feeling that it's some kind of insemination device, but don't know how true that might be.

I don't know if this happened recently or years ago. I've been pregnant twice and lost the baby both times, but I don't know if that's connected. Each time I miscarried, there were perfectly normal reasons for it. The memory is very clear and there's little doubt in my mind that this is a fragment of something real.

I plan to bring this up to the group, but I wanted to let you know about it ahead of time. We may speak privately about this in the future.

Note from Sara: Written December, 1997

This particular conscious memory haunted me more than any other. I thought about it for months. The images were so clear and I could feel everything that had happened to me all over again.

It took months before I could talk about it to the group. When I finally did, I felt relieved and the memory is no longer a part of my everyday thoughts.

Note from Constance:

Interestingly enough, when Sara did bring this incident up in group, it opened the gate for Theresa and Kay to share embarrassing details of their experiences, as well. That's the beauty of a support group. One member's courage to share gets reinforced as another takes the risk and everyone is rewarded.

One of the greatest gifts to me out of this whole experience has been the level of emotional intimacy the Friday Night Group has been able to achieve. The warmth, humor, and openness of these people make each session memorable. Although we all care deeply about one another, the group has developed no common mind set. All have remained seekers of their own truth. Perhaps this is the formula for our success.

All I can say is that Sara's story gives me hope. Her response to her experiences has been inspiring to witness. Because she gained her awareness by having the courage to literally open her eyes and look at what was frightening her, she has been empowered as a result. Most of us dread facing some inner truth about ourselves and we put it out of our awareness until it starts waking us up from our sleep, but can you imagine being awakened by some outer truth? Something beyond your ability to comprehend?

In any given situation in life, we can choose out of love or we can choose out of fear. Sara, determined to learn from her encounters, chose out of love and turned her nightmares into challenges. Hers is the hero's journey. Sara has truly taken one small step for humankind and I hope she is there to calm me if my turn comes to go.

Chapter Eight

We are Not Alone

Kay's Comments On Her Relationship With Lydia
Written: December 1997

During the summer of 1995, I met a fellow experiencer through our therapist, Constance Clear. I told her how I wanted to meet other people like myself. At the same time Constance was counseling me, she was also counseling Lydia. Lydia also expressed a desire to meet someone like herself.

The first time we talked was on the telephone. We found out that we lived only 90 miles apart. We talked for a long time. As the conversation went along, I had the feeling I already knew her. Between the time we talked on the phone and were able to meet in person, I had already put her face with her voice. When we met each other in person, I felt like I was meeting a long lost relative. She was so familiar to me as if we had known each other much longer. I felt a bond between us that I have never felt with a stranger before. Our husbands are both easy going men and got along well together.

Since that summer Lydia has moved much further away, but we do keep in touch with letters and telephone calls. When I call Lydia to tell her about an experience I am having, she will say, "Me too." The same thing happens when she calls me. We usually have experiences at the same time and describe the same ships, aliens, and things on the ships. One object we both described seeing was a clipboard that the aliens carry around with them. The clipboards are made out of what looks like a clear plastic material. They seem to be hand-held computers, but look just like a standard size clipboard.

Lydia and I even get bruises, rashes, and other physical symptoms at the same time and same place on our bodies. We now know we have seen each other during our visits with the aliens, and have known the same alien counselor up there. When he died both of us were in mourning over his death. I miss him so much because he knew me so well, having been with me since birth. I knew it was his time to go because he was so old and he was very tired. His understanding of the human race was exceptional. He was born with a gift of understanding of all races, not just ours. He had an understanding of the soul, more than the outer person he saw. He had the ability to listen to whatever you said and make you feel comfortable.

Lydia once mentioned how our counselor had given her a hug. The next time I saw him, I asked why he hugged Lydia and never hugged me. He said because Lydia needs it and you don't. I then told him I wanted a hug anyway, and he just chuckled and gave me a hug. I remember him with fondness and will never forget him. I am grateful for his kindness.

I have the feeling that Lydia and I are going to continue to be friends for a very long time.

Comments About the Group
Kay:

This is the first support group of any kind that I have attended and I have not been disappointed. It is so great to be able to relate to other people about what happens to me. Everyone understands because they have been through the same thing or something similar to it. Everyone is supportive and non-judgmental of each other. We all seem to fit together so well and the meetings just flow right along. There have been a couple of times when I was unable to go to a meeting and I ended up thinking about them all evening. When someone is missing from the group, I miss them and look at their chair, wishing they were with us.

But none of this would be possible without the loving guidance of our group facilitator, Constance Clear. I think of her as the glue that holds the group together. She is our foundation and support beam. When she starts off the meeting, she emits an energy that helps give me the strength to talk about things that need to be said. I believe she was chosen by the aliens for us because they know how good she is with understanding people. I believe we have been chosen to participate in this group by the aliens. They know we need moral support from each other and the help of an understanding therapist.

This all makes their job a lot easier when we are calmer during the abduction.

If you can find a support group or start one of your own, then by all means do so. It has been a joy to be associated with the members of the Friday Night group. I look forward to our meetings with anticipation of what we will talk about and in seeing everyone.

Daniel:

When we found the group, I was adrift, without a real goal in life, and near the end of my rope, if you will forgive the mixed metaphors. Depression had nearly overwhelmed me, with Prozac a slender plank to clutch in a sea of tears. I still had no real explanation for the depression, other than some people don't make the chemicals needed to counteract depression. I'd left one career and was in college, still uncertain about what the future would hold when I finished the degree. I won't claim that the situation was critical, or that I couldn't have found a resolution in some other way, but I will claim that finding the group has been one of the most significant events of my life.

Something was threatening me, be it run-of-the-mill insanity or alien abduction and I needed help. In the group, we found warm, comforting people who will listen to accounts without a shred of judgment, accepting what we said, questioning only the details in an attempt to further understand what is taking place. We found people with similar troubles, to whom we could offer our strength and understanding, in the process aiding our own healing. If you have energy to offer others, you find the energy you need for yourself. These people are our friends, our confidants, our compatriots in a journey that may never end , or may end in revelations not yet dreamed of by Humans. Their companionship has converted a dark horror-filled travail into a thrilling, still frightening, but no longer oppressive, odyssey.

Today, I have finished my degree, added some additional qualifications, and started a completely different career, one that promises to be more rewarding than I would ever have imagined possible. The depression has lifted and I am stronger than I've been in years. The abduction experience is still there, a lurking presence that I've grown to accept as "normal," much as one might accept baldness as unpleasant but normal, manageable. Life goes on, and it's been vastly more wonderful through knowing and working with our fellow members of the group.

Sara:

When we first met as a group, I didn't know what to expect but when Daniel and I left, I knew from the depth of my heart that this group was going to make an impact to change our lives forever.

As I am writing this, a swell of emotion brings tears to my eyes because I realize these people have never judged anything we have ever said, no matter how crazy we may sound. We accepted each other on our own merit, and gave each other the support we needed. Many times when we didn't have anything to report on our alien activity, we would just talk about other things that were happening in our lives. We solved many of the world's problems during those meetings.

We have become a family and if one of us ever needs help or support we would be there faster than the speed of light.

The group has helped me in many ways. It gave me energy and comfort when I needed it. I no longer fear 3:00 in the morning , or the dark. Getting over the fear of the aliens has helped me get over other fears I have in my daily life. In one of my experiences with the aliens, I made myself look into those big black eyes so that I could deal with the power they had over me for so long. I am working on not letting people in positions of power intimidate me. They can no longer compete with the deep, black eyes of the aliens, a threat I can conquer.

The most important thing about our group is when we open our hearts, souls, and become vulnerable. We do not judge or intrude on anyone's weakness for our own benefit. We support, comfort, question, and give love when needed.

If you can find a group that is supportive, and not simply seeking to hear stories of abduction out of idle or prurient curiosity, you will be on your way to understanding your own alien experience. When seeking a group, keep your mind and heart open. Listen to what people are saying, and if your mind and heart agree, you have found a group that can help you find yourself.

Thank you for reading our stories. Writing our stories has been a therapeutic group effort to explore our own alien experiences. It has been important to let you, the reader, and maybe an abductee, know, "YOU ARE NOT ALONE."

Maggie:

It is very difficult to express in words, the gratitude I feel for our Friday Night Group, and for the immense support of our therapist and dear friend Constance Clear.

Participation in a group like this has helped unmask my life and the horrors I have experienced. It feels great to share with others, who have walked my walk. I do not feel intimidated speaking out in our group, about any of my experiences. It is a comfort to interact.

Finally, Constance Clear's open-minded willingness to speak out on the topic of alien abductions, has been a blessing to me. Thank you very much, Constance and colleagues for being here for me. I love all of you. We have been blessed having Constance Clear accompany us down our dreary paths.

Conclusion

Working on this project has been enormously fulfilling. Not only have I found my clients to be responsive to treatment and the subject matter to be intriguing, but being with the Friday Night Group has become the highlight of every month. I don't know how they manage, but each of the group members maintains a sense of humor in the face of his or her ongoing traumatic encounters.

Unfortunately, not every therapist is able or willing to listen to stories of alien abduction. According to research published by Caroline McLeod Ph.D., Director of Research at PEER, 34 percent of the respondents in her sample who had disclosed their experiences to a therapist found that the topic was dismissed and that their feelings about their experiences were not addressed. Fourteen percent of the respondents reported that disclosure was harmful, in that the therapist either imposed a label of sexual abuse on the experience or displayed more interest in the abduction material than in the person reporting it. The remaining 52 percent of the sample found disclosure to be beneficial. These respondents stated that knowing they were not alone was extremely helpful, and "a number of them noted that the caring presence of the counselor made a life-saving difference."*

It's bad enough that any person would have to endure the helplessness of an alien abduction, but having to maintain silence about it is cruel and debilitating. Even our returning Vietnam veterans had a warm response from society compared to the way people reporting UFO encounters have been treated. Part of the problem is that in our culture, when it comes to the subject of UFO's, you're either considered a skeptic or a true believer. I don't know which is worse. A true believer loses his or her credibility, but a skeptic can't believe in anything.

* McLeod, Caroline, Extraordinary Experience Research at PEER, *CenterPiece*, Issue No. 6, Winter 1995/1996, p. 126.

There's got to be a better way! I recently met a man on an airplane who said he was a "Change Consultant" for the government. I was encouraged to learn that our government employs people with such titles. Although he remained elusive about his duties, we had an interesting discussion about UFO's, and before we landed he explained Change Theory to me.

"It's 10-30-60," he said. "Ten percent of the population will never accept a new paradigm no matter what you do, thirty percent will accept it when you give them rational evidence, and you need the thirty percent to help with the sixty percent."

I hope that in reading these stories you have found enough "rational evidence" to join the thirty percent. Bottom line, something is happening to these people and they need support from the rest of us. The future of humanity may depend on the findings of *whatever* is studying us. Shouldn't we be taking better care of those they are studying?

Appendix A:

Sample Hypnotic Induction

Note from Constance:

For therapists or researchers interested in the technique I use to induce trance, I have included the transcript of the induction portion of the session I held with Andrew on January 17, 1997. Those familiar with hypnosis, will recognize the influence of Milton Erickson, M.D. whose nondirective approach, and deep respect for the unconscious mind, I endeavor to emulate.

Constance: Just letting yourself drift into a comfortable place. Be aware of your body. Let all of your muscles relax. Feeling free to shift or move at any time, so that you can be more comfortable.

By now this must be very familiar for you. Just letting yourself ease down to a comfortable level of relaxation knowing that your conscious mind still has questions. Your unconscious mind is able and willing to assist your conscious mind in exploring, trusting that the unconscious mind will screen that which is important for you to remember and will assist us in ways that we may not understand.

While I'm talking, using my voice as a catalyst, feeling free not to listen to my words, just to let yourself find your own comfortable, relaxed state of being. So comfortable, feeling so good to be alive. Feet relaxing, your lower legs, your knees. And it feels so good to let that tension just dissolve away, all the way up through your buttocks, your upper legs to your abdomen, taking a moment to bathe your kidneys in white light. Healing energy. Allowing your body to heal itself as your relax your lower back, your middle back, your upper back, your shoulders, and your neck. Your abdomen, your diaphragm, your chest, your neck, again relaxing. Down your arms, down through your elbows, your wrists, your hands, your fingers, your scalp. All those muscles in your forehead beginning to relax. Just let your forehead feel smooth. No worries. Just smooth like a baby's forehead. Muscles in

213

your face beginning to relax, your cheeks, your jaw, tongue. Everything is so comfortable, so relaxed.

And as usual, knowing that if there is any extraneous sound that you need to attend to, you will, but otherwise, any sound in the room will just be an invitation to go further and deeper, and deeper and further into your own healing state of relaxation, your own personal place where you can just be and rest and remember, knowing that everything you've ever experienced is recorded through our various senses. Sometimes through bodily sensations, sometimes through visual impressions or images, sometimes through sounds or words or thoughts, sometimes through smells or even tastes. We have various ways of recording our experiences so that they can then be later recalled as is helpful or necessary to do. And in all of our exploration, there are still a couple of areas that remain mysterious.

Letting your unconscious mind choose among those areas, those areas where you have questions so that the experience most important to remember begins to come into your mind, going back in time, back through some of these experiences you've been having in the last several weeks.

Letting your unconscious mind select and choose where to begin. I don't know if you want to go back to where you last left off. If there is other information wanting to come through, just let whatever images that come to mind, come. Just sift through them like you would sift through debris from the river bottom, looking for nuggets of gold. Letting what's waste flow away and what is important or of value remain in your sieve, sifting your experiences, looking for that which is of value, that which is of value to you to remember.

Remembering always that we are doing this work in order that you might feel more comfortable, be more relaxed, feel more reconciled to your experiences, understand better what is happening to you, receive whatever messages are important for you to receive, communicate and write what you see, draw what you see so that others might then benefit from the information that you are receiving.

So relaxed, so very relaxed. Just totally comfortable. Scanning your body to see if there is any part of your body that needs attention, that wants to shift or move or stretch.

And knowing, that, as always, should you need to come out of trance at any point in time, feel free to do so by simply opening your eyes. Otherwise, I'll bring you out gradually when it's time to stop. Just letting yourself go back to where you need to go.

Appendix B:

Could This be Happening to You?

In order to help the reader answer this question, I have included a summary of the results of a survey published by the Roper Organization in 1992, titled *Unusual Personal Experiences.* With 5,947 American adults participating. The survey had a margin of error of plus or minus 1.4%. The report was "the collective effort of a professor of psychiatry at Harvard Medical School, an associate professor of history at Temple University, a psychiatric therapist in Springfield, Missouri, an author and researcher from New York City, and a large polling organization."*

The findings, mailed out to nearly one hundred thousand mental health professionals, were remarkable. In looking at the relation between unusual personal experiences referenced below, and what can be called the "UFO abduction syndrome," the Roper Survey "suggests that hundreds of thousands, if not millions of American men, women and children may have experienced UFO abduction, or abduction related phenomena."

According to the Roper Survey, there is a strong possibility that an individual is a UFO abductee if they answer yes to at least four of five questions having to do with the following experiences:

1. Waking up paralyzed sensing a presence in the room;

2. Feeling as though you are flying through the air;

3. Experiencing an hour or more of missing time;

4. Seeing lights or balls of light in a room without being able to determine their origin; and

5. Finding scars on your body that no one can explain.

Unusual Personal Experiences, An analysis of the data from three major surveys conducted by The Roper Organization, 1992, Bigelow Holding Corp., Las Vegas, Nevada.

Appendix C:

Kay's Suggestions for Abductees:

• Find a competent therapist. A therapist who is willing to work with an abductee is a blessing. I had to learn to live with the aliens in my life. I knew they were here to stay and so was I. The therapy helped beyond what I thought was possible for myself. One of the things therapy did was help me lose weight. I felt like I had no control over my life and my eating was out of control also. In the first year of therapy, I lost 30 pounds without dieting. Therapy gave me hope, and with that hope came a new energy that I had not had in a very long time. In the beginning, I was going every 2 weeks, but now I go only once a month. The 300-mile round trip is well worth the time and effort.

• Find a support group to attend or start one yourself. The great thing about a support group is just what it says in the name. You are supported by others like yourself.

• Try not to forget that they are biological beings the same as we are. We were all created by the same God even though we look and think differently.

• Try to talk to them if you can. It will help you to get over your fear of them. The hardest part for me was to look at their eyes. Once I did that I am now able to look at them and communicate with them just like I were talking to anyone here. Recently I have been complaining to them about how tired I am of their visits and how they are getting me for free. I told them it's time for a trade. They can have me as long as I am not tired the next day because I have to work. That little deal seems to be working so far.

• Don't think you are alone because there are many of us out here. We just need to find a way to connect up with each other. I would love to hear any suggestions on how this can be accomplished.

• I am not a therapist and don't feel comfortable giving advice on what someone should do. All I can do is talk about what I have done for myself and hope it may help someone. Everyone must find their own way and do what they have to in order to make as normal a life as they can for themselves and their families.

Appendix D:

Resource Page

The contributors to this book have agreed to receive mail. Please do not send original documents or anything that you wish to have returned. To write to any of them, include their name on the envelope and send your letter in care of:

c/o **Consciousness Now, Inc.**
P.O. Box 15994
San Antonio, Texas 78212

You may also contact us at our website:
www.reachingforreality.com
or by email: **info@reachingforreality.com**

To locate a therapist, participate in the therapist referral network, or learn about ongoing research at PEER, (the Program For Extraordinary Experience Research founded by John E. Mack, M.D.), write to:

PEER
1493 Cambridge St.
Cambridge, MA 02139
617/497-2667

Other Resources:

Intruder Foundation
Budd Hopkins
P.O. Box 30233
New York, NY 10011

International Center for
Abduction Research
David Jacobs
Dept. of History-Temple Univ.
Philadelphia, PA 19122

Index

A

abductees: alien access to, 18, 27, 105, 111, 185; demographics of, 2, 5, 23, 35-36, 71-73, 89, 179-180, 191-192, 205; encounter with other human abductees, 47, 48, 50, 57, 58, 68, 92, 201; familiarity with other abductees, 23-24, 205-206; family members/friends abduction experiences, 8, 10, 11, 37, 38, 54, 72, 76, 192-194; having children, 5, 7; mourning death of an alien counselor, 31, 206; performing alien tasks, 57-58, 197, 198

Abduction: Human Encounters With Aliens, 12

abduction experiences, physical symptoms of: biopsy-type lesions, 175; "bite marks," 65; blood blisters, 20; blood on bedding, 27, 28, 150, 170; bruises, 27, 28, 32, 205; burn marks, 141; crescent-shaped marks on skin, 25; drugged feeling, 81; elevated lymphocyte count, 175; fatigue/poor sleep, 6, 15, 35, 37, 64, 65, 109, 191-192; hand tremors, 152, 153, 167, 178; headaches, 110, 111, 151, 152, 170, 175, 178, 193; inability to have children, 7, 48; injection sites, 65; joint pains, 109; marks on skin, 3, 73, 141, 145, 170, 171, 175; missing mole, 109, 110; nosebleeds, 150, 152, 188; perfect circle scabs, 74, 77, 78; puncture marks, 31; rashes, 31, 109, 110, 205; rectangular marks/wounds, 84-85, 115; scars, 7, 111; scoop marks, 8, 32, 52, 69; simultaneous symptoms between abductees, 205-206; sinking spells, 152; taste, 67

abduction experiences, psychological symptoms of: absence of, 71; affection/lack of affection toward abductors, 6, 13, 15-16, 39, 63, 64, 68, 69, 130, 148, 206; anxiety, 20, 89, 104, 111, 132, 145, 152, 167, 178, 191, 192, 193, 194; bizarre events ignored, 11, 38, 193; bright lights, fear of, 8; claustrophobia, 32, 191, 192; closets/closet doors, fear of, 60, 61, 62, 192; concentration problems, 7; crowds, fear of, 32; dark, fear of the, 191, 192; depression, 20, 31, 32, 35, 37-38, 89, 104, 111, 178, 192, 207;

219

procedures performed by aliens/abductors

alien book of abductee's experiences and procedures, 157

alien counselor, 13, 31, 206

alien ship, 9, 31, 53, 76-77, 96, 96, 107, 107, 113, 115, 127, 127, 162, 163, 163, 164, 172, 172

alien ship environment and equipment: ability to avoid airplanes, 107; blinking diamond shape, 76-77; blue fluid storage compartments, 143, 143, 144, 158, 160; bright lights, 132, 133, 134, 134, 135; brightly lit rooms, 45, 100, 103; dark liquid, 121-122, 136; dentist's chair, 45, 47, 58, 106, 163, 163; disintegrating ray, 127, 128; engine, 107, 107; enormous hangar, 41, 50-51; equipment failure, 103; exam rooms, 63, 68, 121, 125, 133, 147, 148, 149; exam tables, 62, 67, 92, 93, 93, 100, 113, 149, 201; hatchways, 43, 47; hieroglyphics, 98, 98, 132, 132, 145, 146, 146; instrument console, 46; iron lung-like equipment, 109, 109; keyboard, 57; mall-like area, 68; massive buildings, 124, 124; merry go round of hybrids, 159, 159; return chamber, 149; rooms, large/huge, 41, 42, 43, 45, 50, 57, 92, 92, 108, 108, 109; smells of, 92, 97, 100, 125, 161; tiled areas, 42, 48; time-altering machine, 103, 103, 144; van, interior of, 80; waiting rooms, 50, 58; white and sterile rooms, 50, 194, 200

alien-human hybrids. See hybrid/half alien, half humans

aliens/abductors, behaviors of: brainwashing, 143, 160, 161; broken promise to abductee, 151; concern with taking human samples, 140; curious about abductee's feelings, 148, 194; fear of another alien, 93; indifference, 123, 129, 130, 136-137; lack of understanding human feelings, 142, 149; lying to abductee, 144, 161; mathematical thinking, 136; mean ones, 11, 14, 93; "nicer ones," 14; no feelings, 118-120, 129, 130, 135, 135, 136; no malice toward abductees, 137; organization/ranks of, 148; regrets about injury to abductee, 116; short-tempered, 11; threat of punishment, 48, 49, 93; unnatural interest in human biology, 37

aliens/abductors, death of, 31, 206

aliens/abductors, physical characteristics of: absence of breasts/nipples, 177; appearance changes, 114; baby alien hybrid features, 144, 144; bald/lack of hair, 27, 30, 93, 93; black hair

B

C

closets as places for abduction transport, 20, 60-61, 62

clothing of abductees: pajamas, 13, 41, 43, 55; removed, 51, 56, 62, 92, 97, 100, 103, 106, 109, 112, 114, 125, 133, 138, 145, 151, 158, 168, 174; replaced incorrectly, 67, 85, 96, 99, 152

communication between aliens/abductors and abductees: abductee "knowing," 45; alien picture book of encounters, 158; as an impression, 46; brainwashing, 143, 160-161; by formula and math figures, 98, 98, 116-120, 122, 123, 123, 131, 132, 132; intrusive thoughts, 75, 77, 78; message through feeling, 194; sense of a decision to obey aliens, 49; sense of an unspoken message, 55; staring, 56, 58; telepathic, 12, 78, 92, 100, 103, 159-160, 174, 196, 198, 199, 201; threat of punishment, 48, 49, 93; unexpected tap on forehead, 46-47

Communion, 24, 25, 35, 188, 192

Consciousness Now, Inc., 217

Cyan, 95, 98, 158

D

devils inside, alien experience viewed as, 180

"dimensions of sight and non-sight," 114, 115, 142, 144

disintegrating ray, 127, 127, 128, 129, 132

dogs: abducted and on alien ship, 114, 115, 126, 129; response to alien presence, 64, 65, 96, 99, 108, 162, 164, 176, 186

dreams/nightmares of abduction experiences, 7, 17-18, 19, 25, 26, 28, 30, 43, 59, 60, 63, 73, 78, 79, 79, 80, 89, 95, 104, 141, 150, 152, 157, 158, 168, 171, 176, 178, 195, 202

dual reality of abductees, 21, 51

E

Erickson, Milton, 213

F

female aliens, 11, 12, 13-14, 28, 30, 30, 147, 148, 148, 149, 151, 151, 153, 176, 176

Fire in the Sky, 87

formulas and math figures viewed by abductees, 116-120, 122, 123, 123, 131, 132, 132

Friday Night Group, 1, 84, 86, 105, 167, 179, 191, 199, 203, 205-209, 211

From Elsewhere: Being ET in America, 16

G

ghosts or spirits, alien experience viewed as, 7, 12, 25, 26, 89, 91-95, 181, 182, 185, 186

Grays, 11, 14, 27, 28, 47, 55, 56, 57, 58, 63, 68, 69, 93, 100, 109, 162, 164, 170, 175, 176, 178, 194, 195, 196, 200, 201, 202

gun next to bed after abduction experience, 105, 108, 162, 164

H

Harbor, The, 191

Healing Shattered Reality, 75

hieroglyphics, 98, 98, 132, 132, 145, 146, 146

holographic alien, sighting of, 74-76, 151

Hopkins, Budd, 192

human death, becoming an alien, 161

hybrid/half-alien, half-humans, 31, 32, 143, 144, 158, 158, 159, 159, 160, 160, 176, 176, 177

94, 94, 140; suction cups to body parts, 112, 112; symphonic noise placed in brain, 78; to throat, 15, 31; tissue removal/biopsies, 25, 31, 94, 95, 101; urine samples, 62; "X's and O's, removal of, 19

T

U

V

W

Z

About the Author

Constance Clear is a lecturer and psychotherapist with a Master of Arts degree in psychology from Trinity University and a Masters of Social Work degree from Our Lady of the Lake University. She has been in private practice since 1976, working with individuals, couples, and families. After fifteen years of facilitating a support group for bereaved parents, Constance began to study the UFO phenomena, which led to her working with abductees and culminated in the creation of this book. Her credentials include: L.M.S.W.-A.C.P., L.M.F.T., A.C.S.W., and B.C.D..

Order Form

Name _____

Address _____

City _____ State _____ Zip _____

Phone _____ Email _____

Please send me _____ copies of "Reaching For Reality", for $16.95 each plus $3.00 each shipping and handling.

❏ Check ❏ Money Order ❏ VISA ❏ MasterCard ❏ AMEX

Card Number _____ Exp Date _____

Texas residents please add 7.75% sales tax.

Mail this order form to:

Consciousness Now, Inc.
P.O. Box 15994
San Antonio, TX 78212

You may also order "Reaching For Reality" at our website:
http://www.reachingforreality.com

or by calling

1 (800) 507-BOOK (2665)